NATIONAL BUSINESS SPELLER

BY

BENJAMIN J. CAMPBELL

AUTHOR OF

DRILLS IN CORRECT ENGLISH
MODERN BUSINESS PUNCTUATION

JOINT AUTHOR OF

BRIEF BUSINESS ENGLISH
ESSENTIALS OF BUSINESS ENGLISH
BUSINESS LETTERS: HOW TO WRITE THEM

AND

BRUCE L. VASS

JOINT AUTHOR OF

BRIEF BUSINESS ENGLISH
ESSENTIALS OF BUSINESS ENGLISH
BUSINESS LETTERS: HOW TO WRITE THEM

BUSINESS ENGLISH PUBLISHING COMPANY
JACKSON, MICHIGAN

PREFACE

It is generally conceded that the results secured in spelling have not been satisfactory. This is due, in a large measure, to the fact that heretofore it has been necessary to learn each word separately. The National Business Speller presents a few simple principles, which can be easily mastered, that govern the spelling of thousands of words.

For example, there are more than a thousand words ending in *able* and *ible*, about four hundred of which are common. To learn these words separately is a prodigious task. The National Business Speller gives simple tests for determining how to spell words of this class.

Simple tests are also given that make easy the spelling of words ending in *ous* and *us*, *cal* and *cle*, *ise* and *ize*, *cial* and *tial*—classes of words that have heretofore been very difficult. Then, too, the Law of Association, that invaluable aid to memory, is used to eliminate all difficulty in spelling a large number of words that otherwise are particularly troublesome.

Thus, it will be seen that in the National Business Speller whole groups of words are so classified that they may be learned according to certain principles—something that has never before been done.

Ayres' list of 1,000 most commonly used words, Thorndike's list of 10,000 words, and Jones' list of 100 "demons" have been searched, and all the words suitable for a book of this nature have been included in this text.

In the preparation of this text, two classes of words have been studiously avoided:

First, those words, of which there are a great many, that present no difficulty in spelling, and which, therefore, should find no place in a book of this kind.

Second, those words, usually found in large numbers in spelling books, that belong only to the dictionary. This class includes words rarely used in business or social intercourse. Many of them belong only to the vocabulary of the specialist, and should be learned only as they are needed. As an example of this class of words, we submit the follow-

iii

ing words from well-known spelling books: *umbrageous, endogenous, aileron, calligraphy, lapis lazuli.* Such words find no place in the National Business Speller.

That words to be learned should be presented as nearly as possible as they appear in ordinary use is generally conceded by educators. But strict adherence to this principle would sacrifice syllabication— that other great aid to spelling. It is undesirable to respell more than is necessary to show the pronunciation, for in respelling, incorrect forms are placed before the eye of the pupil. In this text, only those words have been respelled about which there might be doubt as to the pronunciation. The words have been divided into syllables and the accented syllable marked, but in order to present the words as nearly as possible in the way they usually appear, hyphens have not been inserted between the syllables.

The spelling, pronunciation, and syllabication of the words in this text are in accordance with Webster's New International Dictionary. The definitions, though necessarily brief, will be found sufficiently comprehensive to make clear the meaning of the words. Whenever possible, synonyms have been used as definitions.

The value of frequent reviews should not be overlooked. In fact, the daily review of a few words from preceding lessons will multiply many times over the effectiveness of the methods presented in this speller.

Rules for Spelling

The mastery of a few simple principles of word building will greatly lessen the work necessary to become a good speller. For example, there are about five thousand words that end in final *e* silent. The average student can, without preparation, spell 99% of all these words. The difficulty arises when suffixes are added. A mastery of a simple principle of word building, together with about a dozen exceptions, eliminates this difficulty.

A few other rules, applying to smaller groups of words, are also invaluable.

Silent *e* Dropped

Rule 1—Words ending in silent *e* drop the *e* before a suffix beginning with a vowel, except words ending in *ce* or *ge* followed by *able* or *ous;* as, *use, using, usable, usage; move, moving, movable; sale, salable; guide, guidance.* (See Lesson 24.)

Note—Since *c* and *g* always have the hard sound before *a* and *o*, words ending in *ce* or *ge* retain final *e* before the suffix *able* or *ous* in order to preserve the soft sound of *c* and *g;* as, *change, changeable; courage, courageous; outrage, outrageous; peace, peaceable.*

Silent *e* Retained

Rule 2—Words ending in silent *e* retain the *e* before a suffix beginning with a consonant; as, *use, useful, useless; move, movement; definite, definitely.* (See Lesson 25.)

Final Consonant Doubled

Rule 3—Monosyllables and words of more than one syllable accented on the last syllable, ending in a single consonant, preceded by a single vowel, double the final consonant on taking a suffix beginning with a vowel; as, *rob, robber, robbing, robbed; remit, remitted, remitting, remittance.* (See Lesson 28.)

Words Ending in *y*

Rule 4—Words ending in *y* preceded by a consonant change the *y* to *i* before any suffix except one beginning with *i;* as, *signify, signified, signifies, significant; accompany, accompanied, accompanies, accompaniment.* (See Lesson 38.)

Plurals

Rule 5—Nouns regularly form their plurals by adding *s*, but *es* is added when the word is easier to pronounce than it would be with *s;* as, *book, books; bench, benches.*

Rule 6—Nouns ending in *y* preceded by a consonant form their plurals by changing the *y* to *i* and adding *es;* as, *lady, ladies; company, companies.*

Rule 7—Nouns ending in *y* preceded by a vowel form their plurals by adding *s;* as, *valley, valleys; turkey, turkeys; holiday, holidays.*

Rule 8—Nouns ending in *o* preceded by a vowel form their plurals by adding *s;* as, *cameo, cameos; folio, folios.*

Rule 9—Nouns ending in *o* preceded by a consonant form their plurals by adding *s* or *es;* as, *piano, pianos; calico, calicoes.*

Rule 10—Most nouns ending in *f* or *fe* form their plurals by adding *s;* but a few nouns change the *f* or *fe* to *ves;* as, *brief, briefs; proof, proofs; loaf, loaves; leaf, leaves.* (See Lesson 39.)

General Principles Governing Pronunciation

C and *g* usually have the hard sound before *a, o,* and *u;* as, *cable, gable, cottage, gone, cutter, gutter.*

C and *g* usually have the soft sound before *e, i,* and *y,* as, *cede, gender, cinder, ginger, cycle, gymnasium.*

A vowel at the end of an accented syllable is usually long; as, *fa′vor, re′cent, ri′val, ro′ta ry, stu′dent.*

A vowel is usually long if before a single consonant followed by silent *e;* as, *made, mete, mite, note, cute.*

A vowel is usually long if it stands alone in an accented syllable; as, *a′gent, i′ci cle, o′men, e′ther, u′nit.*

A vowel is usually short if at the beginning of an accented syllable; as, *at′ti tude, es′ti mate, in′ti mate, op′er ate, up′per.*

A vowel is usually short in the middle of an accented syllable unless the syllable ends with silent *e;* as, *bat′ter y, for get′ful, lot′ter y, lit′er al, Co lum′bi a.*

Guide to Pronunciation

LONG VOWELS

ā   *as in* pāle, chāos, lābor.
ē   "   ēven, scēne, serēne.
ī   "   īce, inspīre, delīght.
ō   "   ōld, hōpe, herō, calicō.
ū   "   ūse, tūne, dūty, hūman.
o͞o   "   mo͞on, fo͞od, to͞ol, bo͞ot.

Note—Long Vowels usually occur in accented syllables.

SHORT VOWELS

ă   *as in* ăm, ădd, ăccept.
ĕ   "   ĕnd, mĕt, ĕfface.
ĭ   "   belĭttle, habĭt.
ŏ   "   ŏdd, nŏt, cŏttage.
ŭ   "   ŭp, cŭtter, stŭdy.
o͝o   "   go͝od, co͝ok, bo͝ok.

MODIFIED LONG VOWELS

ȧ   *as in* senȧte, prefȧce, delicȧte.
ė   "   ėvent, crėate, serėne.
ȯ   "   ȯbey, anatȯmy, prȯpose.
ů   "   ůnite, formůlate, hůmane.

Note—Modified Long Vowels usually occur in unaccented syllables.

OBSCURE VOWELS

ȃ   *as in* finȃl, madȃm, infȃnt.
ȧ   "   sofȧ, ideȧ, ȧbound.
ȇ   "   recȇnt, decȇnt, novȇl.
ȏ   "   cȏnnect, cȏntrol.
ȗ   "   caucȗs, circȗs, focȗs.

Note—Obscure vowels usually occur in unaccented syllables only.

OTHER VOWELS AND DIPHTHONGS

â   *as in* câre, compâre, pârent.
ä   "   färther, pälm, cälm, fär.
ȧ   "   grȧss, stȧff, dȧnce, pȧth.
ē̇   "   pē̇rvert, ē̇rmine, gē̇rm.
ô   "   ôrder, bôught, côrk, ôrb.

û   *as in* ûrn, concûr, ûrge, fûr.
ü   "   French and German words, menu, Sünde.
oi, oy, *as in* boil, oil, boy.
ou, ow, "   out, trout, vow.

OTHER SIGNS USED IN RESPELLING

ŋ   (like ng) *as in* iŋk, baŋk, raŋkle.
N   A small capital *n* (thus N) is used in respelling to indicate that a preceding vowel is pronounced as a nasal, as in French boN.
t̬ů   used to indicate the changing of *t* to *ch*, *as in* cult̬ůre, legislat̬ůre, pict̬ůre.
d̬ů   used to indicate the changing of *d* to *j* as in grad̬ůal, grand̬eur, verd̬ůre.
th   *as in* thin, thick, through, loath.
th   "   though, breathe, there, then.

CONTENTS

viii

LESSON 1

de vel'op, to unfold; to grow; to come to light gradually.

ex plic'it, exact; especially clear or plain; definite.

rec'i pe, a formula for making some combination or preparation.

man'i fest, to show; apparent.

nor'mal, conforming to a type or standard; natural.

sub side', to lower or sink; to become quiet or calm.

ca'ter, to provide food; to supply what is needed or desired.

u ten'sil, an implement or vessel.

ap prove' (ă prōōv'), to sanction; to commend.

boy'cott, to combine to withhold trade or social intercourse.

tour'na ment (tōōr'-), a series of contested games.

mur'mur, to mutter or grumble.

lime'light, a calcium light; in a conspicuous position.

pag'eant (păj'ĕnt; pā'jĕnt), a stately or showy procession.

re source', available means; natural advantages.

bur'y, to cover up; to inter.

tar'iff, a tax or duty levied on imported or exported goods.

cor're late, to connect through mutual relation.

as tute', keen; shrewd; discerning.

ex'it (ĕk'sĭt), act of departing; a passage out.

ag'gra vate, to make worse or more severe; to intensify.

as so'ci ate (-shĭ āt), a companion; to join with.

ear'nest, serious; ardent; intent in purpose.

ster'ling, standard; genuine.

e lat'ed, exultant; excited; flushed with success.

pet'ty, trifling; trivial; of little importance.

fran'tic, frenzied; wildly excited; distracted.

tur'moil, disturbance; commotion.

as sure' (-shōōr'), to make certain; to convince.

cop'y right, the exclusive right to print, publish, or sell.

ag'i tate, to stir up; to excite; to discuss.

ver'i fy, to prove to be true.

or'na ment, anything that adorns or beautifies; to adorn.

nur'ture, to give nourishment to; that which nourishes.

for'mer, preceding in time or place; previous.

ves'tige (-tĭj), a sign or trace.

pend'ing, not yet decided or finished; awaiting.

bank'rupt, unable to pay debts; one who is bankrupt.

prof'fer, to offer for acceptance.

tal'ent, superior mental ability; special aptitude.

LESSON 2

ab surd′, ridiculous; contrary to reason or sense.

ac′me, the highest point or summit; perfection; climax.

dis tinct′, separate; easily seen or perceived.

ad ja′cent, lying near; adjoining.

chal′lenge, to defy; to object to; act of challenging.

ac crue′ (ă krōō′), to be added as increase or profit.

ad mon′ish, to warn; to reprove gently; to caution.

pur′port, the meaning intended.

ep′i sode, distinct incident; prominent event.

sub′sti tute, a person or thing put in the place of another.

a lign′ment, (-līn-′), act of placing in line.

pal′lid, pale; lacking in color.

bar′ri er, that which hinders or obstructs; a boundary.

con tra dict′, to deny; to oppose in words.

rec′ti fy, to correct; to refine by distillation.

co in cide′, to agree with; concur.

al le′vi ate, to lighten; to make easier to bear.

col′league, an associate or fellow member.

ab nor′mal, unnatural; irregular.

so lu′tion, the act of solving; liquid holding dissolved elements.

ad journ′, to close, as a meeting; to postpone.

knowl′edge (nŏl′ĕj), act or state of knowing; information.

haz′ard, chance; risk; danger; to venture.

tinge, to color slightly; a tint.

con′cen trate, to focus; to intensify; to condense.

ped′es tal, base or support of a column or statue.

da′ta (dā′tà), facts upon which conclusions are based.

to geth′er, not apart; in concert.

de fray′, to pay or discharge, as a debt, costs, etc.

trib′ute, praise; money paid for peace or protection.

ros′ter (rŏs′-), a roll or list of names or members.

a lert′, keenly on the watch.

re sent′ (-zĕnt′), to feel, express, or exhibit displeasure at.

e ject′, to throw out; to evict or dispossess.

seg′re gate, to place apart or to separate.

re plete′, filled; abounding; full.

ac knowl′edge (-nŏl′ĕj), to own or admit to be true.

an′nals, records by years; chronology.

ad′vo cate, a pleader; to plead for.

ag′gre gate, mass: assemblage of parts as a whole.

LESSON 3

det'ri ment, that which injures or reduces in value; injury.

cur'tain (-tĭn), a hanging screen that may be drawn up or aside.

in fringe', to encroach upon, as a patent or copyright.

stig'ma, any mark of disgrace.

u'su ry (ū' zhŭ rĭ), exorbitant or illegal interest.

di vert', to turn aside; deflect; to entertain.

en cour'age, to inspire with courage; to cheer.

cli'max, the highest point; acme.

cel'e brate, to praise; to observe in honor of.

an'i mat ed, full of life; vigorous; lively.

en gross', to copy elaborately; to absorb one's attention.

dis perse', to scatter; to distribute.

ex ces'sive, exceeding what is due; overmuch.

ac'cess, means, place, or way of approach or admission.

prime, first in rank or importance; full perfection.

reg'i ment, a body of troops.

fash'ion, prevailing style; to form or shape.

du'pli cate, an exact copy; twofold; to reproduce exactly.

en ti'tle, to give a right or title to.

has'ten (has"n), to move with speed; to dispatch.

skel'e ton, bony framework of an animal; an outline.

bou quet' (bōō kā'), a bunch of flowers; a nosegay.

fea'ture, any marked characteristic; to give prominence to.

dit'to, the same thing repeated.

op'po site, (-zĭt), over against; facing; contrary.

af front', a deliberately offensive act or word.

man'u al, pertaining to the hand; a handbook.

tac'tics, method of procedure.

ex empt' (ĕg zĕmpt'), free from a duty or obligation.

de mol'ish, to destroy; to reduce to ruins.

ac cu'mu late, to heap or pile up; to amass; to collect.

ar rears', money due and unpaid.

quo'ta, the share assigned to each in a division.

e lab'o rate, perfected; complicated; to work out in detail.

por tray' (pōr-), to draw or paint; to describe vividly.

ax'i om, a self-evident truth.

ban'ish, to exile; to dispel from the mind.

de funct', dead; extinct; without function.

triv'i al, of little worth; trifling.

nov'el ty, something novel or new; an innovation.

LESSON 4

fix'ture, a fixed or permanent appliance or part.

im peach', to charge with misconduct in office; to discredit.

con'fis cate, to seize property for public purposes.

par'cel, a package; a portion.

beck'on (běk''n), to summon by a motion of the hand.

un'der signed, the signer or signers of a document.

piv'ot, a point or pin on which something turns.

re peal', to revoke; to rescind.

suf fice' (-fīs'; -fīz'), to satisfy; to be enough.

ba'sin, a dish or pan; a depression in the land.

de pre'ci ate (-shǐ āt), to lessen in value; to underrate.

at trib'ute, to impute or ascribe.

height (hīt), distance above the base or level.

lat'i tude, distance from the equator; range; scope.

vic'tim, one sacrificed or made to suffer; a dupe.

ef face', to blot out; to erase.

loi'ter, to linger on the way; to spend time idly.

ad'e quate, equal to all requirements; sufficient.

cot'ton, a plant and its fiber.

dig'ni ty, worthiness; position or rank; stately manner.

doc'trine, that which is taught; tenet; principle.

em bar'rass, to disconcert; to involve in financial difficulties.

e mer'gen cy, a sudden crisis or a pressing necessity.

men'ace, a threat; to threaten.

re buff', a curt refusal; repulse; to repel curtly.

de pos'it, to put on deposit in a bank; to lay down.

se'ries (-rēz), a number of things or events in related order.

que'ry, a question; an inquiry.

spe cif'ic, definite or particular; precise.

per'fi dy, breach of faith; disloyalty; treachery.

ran'som (-sŭm), a price for release from captivity.

ex'ca vate, to dig or hollow out.

tract, a religious leaflet; a large area of land.

in voke', to call upon earnestly; to implore.

prej'u dice (-ᴏᴏ dǐs), bias; a premature opinion.

ob'so lete, out of date or use.

con done', to treat as though forgiven or excused.

cov'et (kŭv'ĕt), to desire wrongly and eagerly.

in'di gent, destitute; needy.

cham'pi on, one who has won supremacy; to defend or support.

LESSON 5

de spair´, to give up hope; loss of hope.

con ceal´, to hide; to withhold knowledge of.

i´so late (ī´sŏ lāt; ĭs´ŏ-), to place by itself or alone.

per pet´u al, everlasting; endless.

ho ri´zon, the apparent junction of earth and sky.

def´i cit (-sĭt), a shortage, especially of money.

be ware´, to be on one's guard; to exercise prudence.

en su´ing, following as to time.

min´i mum, the least quantity allowable or permissible.

scath´ing (skāth´-), bitterly severe; as, a *scathing* rebuke.

dray´age, charge for carriage by dray; cartage.

clar´i fy, to make clear or pure.

cus´tom, established usage; a tariff or duty.

dis cern´ (-zûrn´), to perceive and recognize; to discriminate.

hav´oc, wide and general destruction; devastation.

tre´ble (trĕb´'l), threefold; triple.

sig´nal, a sign to give notice; remarkable; to make signals to.

stam´i na, staying power; endurance; strength.

ma jes´tic, stately; dignified.

liq´ui date (lĭk´wĭ dāte), to adjust or settle a debt; to convert into cash.

en vi´ron ment, surrounding conditions or forces.

sig´na ture, a person's name written by himself.

di´a mond (mŭnd), a brilliant precious stone.

re voke´, to recall or to repeal.

pres´sure, force or weight acting against anything.

me´di o cre (-kēr), ordinary; of medium excellence.

ver´bal, pertaining to words; consisting merely of words.

re plen´ish, to fill again.

trust´wor thy, fit or worthy to be trusted; reliable.

con sol´i date, to unite; to make solid or coherent.

in´so lent, insulting; grossly disrespectful.

dis turb´, to agitate; to unsettle.

ten´ta tive, by way of trial; experimental.

con´crete, real; not abstract; a building compound.

re bate´, a payment back; a deduction; to diminish.

tex´ture, characteristic weave.

af fil´i ate, to ally; to unite with; to associate one's self with.

fu´ner al, ceremonies attending the burial of the dead.

glis´ten (glĭs´'n), to sparkle.

car´riage, bearing; demeanor; a vehicle; charge for carrying.

LESSON 6

av′er age, ordinary size or quality; usual; medium.

quo′rum, enough members to transact business legally.

ap pro′pri ate, suitable; set apart for a particular use.

sur′plus, more than is sufficient.

pat′tern, a model; figure or design; to imitate.

pos sess′ (pŏ zĕs′), to own or to have in possession.

so′journ (so′jûrn), to dwell for a time; a short stay.

con cise′, brief; terse; condensed.

knot′ty, with many knots; difficult; puzzling.

dis solve′, to separate; to become liquid by solution.

pa′tri ot (pā′trĭ ŏt; păt′rĭ-), one who loves his country.

de′vi ate, to turn aside from.

mo roc′co, a fine kind of leather made of goatskin.

hand′some (han′sŭm), pleasing to look upon; well-formed; liberal.

dis patch′, to send away in haste; a message.

re′cent, new; late; modern.

en dow′, to supply with a fund or a gift.

rec′ti tude, rightness of principle or practice; uprightness.

nour′ish, to feed or to sustain.

fort′night (fôrt′nīt; nĭt), a period of two weeks.

hap′haz ard, at random; determined by chance.

prob′lem, a difficult matter to be settled or solved.

cope, to contend or strive with, usually on equal terms.

ap plause′, expression of approval.

res′cue, to deliver from danger or harm; to liberate.

re coup′ (-cōōp′), to regain; to reimburse; indemnify.

lev′y, to raise or collect, as by assessment.

post′er, a bill or placard.

it self′, the emphatic or reflexive form of *it.*

ac com′mo date, to oblige; to adjust or adapt.

ex pul′sion, a driving or forcing out; act of expelling.

pre′cept, a rule of conduct.

ex hib′it (ĕg zĭb′ĭt), to present to view; to display.

co erce′, to compel by force or authority; to restrain.

cer′ti fy, to testify to in writing; to verify.

in′stinct, a natural impulse.

weap′on (wĕp′ŭn), something to fight with.

tinc′ture, a tinge or tint; a solution of a drug; to tinge.

ban′quet, an elaborate feast.

foun′tain (-tĭn), a water jet; source of supply.

LESSON 7

ac com′plish, to bring about; to effect; to complete.

con′se quence, a natural or necessary result.

as tound′, to overwhelm with wonder; to confound.

de tect′, to find out or discover.

ab solve′, to clear of crime or guilt; to set free.

for′mu la, a fixed rule; a prescription or recipe.

fa′vor ite (-ĭt), a person or thing preferred.

gran′ite, a hard crystalline rock.

del′e gate, one empowered to act for another; to intrust.

ag grieved′, having a grievance; oppressed.

fer′vor, intensity of feeling; ardor; zeal; warmth.

se′quel, succeeding part or result.

ap′pe tite, desire for or relish of food or drink.

im me′di ate, done at once; adjoining; with nothing between.

pe ruse′ (pĕ rōōz′), to read with care and attention.

se date′, serious; calm; sober.

chores (chōrz), the daily light work of a farm or household.

max′im, a general truth or terse rule of conduct; a proverb.

or′de al, a severe trial or test.

ob ses′sion, the fact or state of being ruled by one idea.

pa thet′ic, exciting pity; touching the feelings.

en hance′, to increase; to advance; to intensify.

thor′ough (thŭr′ō), complete; perfect; finished.

dec′ade, a period of ten years.

cal′i ber, diameter of the bore of a gun; mental capacity.

ad′junct, joined subordinately; an auxiliary.

sure (shōōr), certain; confident; beyond doubt.

op por tune′, timely; seasonable.

suc cumb′ (sŭ kŭm′), to yield; to submit; to give up.

re veal′, to make known; to disclose; to divulge.

af′flu ence, an abundant supply; opulence.

vi cin′i ty, region near or about.

jour′nal, a daily record or register; a newspaper.

con niv′ance, secretly aiding or assenting to wrongdoing.

lei′sure (lē′zhŭr), freedom from occupation; spare time.

mam′moth, very large; gigantic.

mys′te ry, something secret, unknown, or incomprehensible.

sci′ence, classified knowledge of general truths or general laws.

de plete′, to reduce or exhaust.

pre con ceive′, to conceive or form an idea beforehand.

LESSON 8

va'ry, to alter or change in appearance, shape, etc.

rum'mage, to ransack; to search thoroughly; a thorough search.

clause, a subordinate sentence; a distinctive proviso.

in clem'ent, severe; harsh; stormy.

ze'nith, the point in the heavens directly overhead.

en'mi ty, animosity; ill will; hostility.

a cross', from side to side; crosswise; beyond.

suc'cor (sŭk'ēr), aid; to help.

pen'e trate, to pierce; to comprehend; to discern.

a piece', to or for each person or thing; each; severally.

pri'ma ry, first in rank or importance; principal.

par (pär), equal to face value.

con cern', a business firm; anxiety; to relate to.

mar'gin (-jĭn), the edge or border; a limit.

in frac'tion, act of breaking a law or obligation.

van'guard, troops in front.

re lax', to become lax or less rigid; to slacken.

di vorce', annulment of marriage; separation.

ex tant', still existing; living.

im per'son ate, to act in the character of; to personate.

ex'cerpt, a selected or copied passage or extract.

cir'cu lar, a printed or written letter; a notice; round.

sou ve nir' (sōō vē nēr'; sōō'vĕ-nēr), a keepsake; a memento.

scoun'drel, a rascal; a villain.

ten'der, not tough; sympathetic; to offer for acceptance.

ac cuse', to blame or charge with an offense.

res'pite (-pĭt), a putting off; delay; a reprieve.

ab'sence, state of being absent.

cam paign', a series of operations; a contest.

tem'po ra ry, lasting for a short time only; not permanent.

pre dic'a ment, an embarrassing or perplexing situation.

men'u (mĕn'ū), a bill of fare.

mer'can tile (-tĭl), pertaining to merchants or trade; commercial.

con vene', to come together; to assemble.

se'quence, succession; arrangement; series.

ledg'er, a book of accounts.

an tic'i pate, to expect; to do beforehand.

rai'ment, clothing in general; garments.

lu'cid, clear; mentally sound.

buoy'ant (boi'-), tending to rise or to float; hopeful.

LESSON 9

expediency
expedient

ac cred'it, to give credit to; to authorize.

rel'ish, to like the taste of; flavor, especially when pleasing.

di lute', to make thinner or weaken, as with water.

dis'ci pline, training; to govern.

ran'dom (-dŭm), lack of a definite aim or method; haphazard.

ju've nile (jōō've nĭl; -nīl), immature; young.

frus'trate, to prevent from attaining a purpose; to baffle.

ba'sis, the base or foundation.

con gest', to accumulate at one point; to overcrowd.

in teg'ri ty, uprightness of character; moral soundness.

sce'nic (sē'nĭk), offering fine views of nature.

at'ti tude, posture; mental mood.

dep'u ty, an agent or appointed substitute.

au then'tic, genuine; real; having authority.

at tain', to achieve; to accomplish; to reach.

pre dict', to foretell; prophesy.

pa trol', to walk around in order to guard; a guard.

per son nel', the persons collectively employed in any service.

par'a mount, supreme; chief.

hu mil'i ty, the quality of being humble; meekness.

ex'pe dite, to hasten the progress of; to facilitate.

stam pede', sudden flight through panic; to run away in a panic.

fab'ric, a woven cloth; structure or texture.

ter'ri to ry, a region or district.

in volve', to implicate; to embarrass; to complicate.

con'quer (-kĕr), to overcome; to subdue.

re fus'al, the act of refusing; the right to refuse or reject.

pal'ate, the roof of the mouth.

ob'vi ate, to remove or clear away beforehand; to prevent.

doc'u ment, any writing conveying information or evidence.

gaud'y, (gôd'ĭ), highly colored; showy; flashy.

ten'den cy, trend; inclination.

en act', to make into an act or a law; to decree.

cen'sure, to blame; to criticize adversely.

ded'i cate, to devote solemnly; to consecrate.

hor'ror, great fear; abhorrence.

prop'er, fit; correct; appropriate; becoming.

pre'cinct, a voting district; a place marked off by fixed lines.

spe'cie (-shĭ), coined money.

va ri'e ty, a varied assortment; diversity.

LESSON 10

ef fec′tive, yielding results; efficient; impressive.

ir′ri gate, artificial watering of land by means of canals.

lux′u ry, anything that gives enjoyment, but is not a necessity.

re tal′i ate, to repay evil in kind.

per′me ate, to pervade or pass through the pores of.

ex ag′ger ate (ĕg zăj′ẽr āte), to enlarge beyond the truth.

rev′e nue, income from property; taxes, rents, etc.

ap pease′, to quiet; to pacify.

a pol′o gy, an excuse formally offered; a makeshift.

do′nate, to give, especially to religious or charitable objects.

ul′ti mo, in the month preceding the present.

lad′ing, a load or cargo; freight.

pres′tige (-tĭj), influence based on past achievements.

splen′dor (-dẽr), brilliancy; pomp.

er rat′ic, eccentric; having no certain course; queer.

hom′age (hŏm′-), respect; reverence; honor.

in′ti mate, familiar; to hint.

hu′mor (hū′mẽr; ū′-), to indulge; sense of fun; skin disease.

poise, balance; equilibrium; repose.

mu se′um (mṳ zē′ŭm), a repository for curiosities, works of art, nature, etc.

im pu′ni ty, freedom from punishment, injury, or loss.

com′pen sate, to make a fit return for; to make amends.

fis′cal, pertaining to the public treasury or revenue; financial.

oc′cu py, to hold or to dwell in.

av′e nue, a way or means of approach; a broad street.

bu′reau (-rō), chest of drawers; government department.

ir′ri tate, to provoke or make angry; to inflame.

rav′age, to lay waste; despoil.

re new′, to make new again; to supply anew.

vi′ti ate (vĭsh′ĭ āte), to make impure; to render ineffective.

ven′om (-ŭm), poison, as of serpents, etc.; spite.

res′i due, remainder; what is left.

im por tune′, to urge or plead persistently.

fa nat′ic, a visionary enthusiast.

sum′ma ry, an abstract; done without delay or formality.

de′pot (dē′pō), a storehouse; a railroad station.

en thu′si asm, intense interest.

budg′et (bŭj′ĕt), a financial estimate; package of papers.

vest′ed, fixed, as a right; clothed.

bal′ance, difference between the two sides of an account; to put in equilibrium.

Begins

LESSON 11

spec′i men, a part intended to show the quality of the whole.

ban′ner, any flag or standard; worthy to bear the banner.

flour′ish (flŭr′ĭsh), to thrive; to flaunt or brandish.

con jec′ture, a guess; to surmise.

pos′i tive, certain; leaving no doubt; not negative.

cou′pon (kōō′pŏn), a detachable portion of a bond, ticket, etc.

am′bu lance, a vehicle for conveying the sick or injured.

dras′tic, violent in action; harsh.

cur′ren cy, a circulating medium of exchange; money.

ver′sion, an account from a particular point of view.

ac cus′tomed, familiar through use; customary.

co los′sal, gigantic; enormous.

pat′ent, an exclusive right to use or sell an invention; plain.

ver′sa tile (-tĭl), able to do many things well.

po lice′ (-lēs′), officers for maintaining order.

bi′as, prejudice; obliquely.

prod′i gy, something extraordinary; a marvel; a wonder.

doc′ile (dŏs′ĭl), easily managed; teachable.

per′pe trate, to do or commit.

di plo′ma, an official certificate of graduation.

com′pli cate, to make or become difficult or intricate.

neg′a tive, a photographic image; opposed to affirmative.

gran′deur (-dŭr), magnificence; sublimity; stateliness.

tar′nish, to dim the luster of.

con serve′, to save; to keep from loss or decay.

qual′i ty (kwŏl′-), the nature or property of; high rank.

ven′ture, an undertaking involving risk; to take a chance.

im bue′, to absorb; to saturate.

sa lute′, to greet; to welcome; a sign of respect.

ven′geance (-jăns), retribution; revenge, usually just.

drudg′er y, work that is irksome or distasteful.

del′uge, a flood; to overwhelm.

per spec′tive, appearance as limited by distance or viewpoint.

pen′nant, a long, narrow flag or streamer.

con′strue (-strōō), to explain or to interpret.

lav′ish, profuse; excessive.

va′por, any cloudlike substance floating in the air.

me′di um, middle condition; means or agency.

ul′ti mate, final; extreme; last.

re course′, the person or thing to which one turns for aid.

LESSON 12

di gress′, to turn aside from the main subject; to deviate.

pre serve′, to keep from injury or decay; to protect.

anx i′e ty (ăng zī′ĕ tĭ), troubled uneasiness of mind; solicitude.

su perb′, grand; elegant; stately.

laun′der, to wash and iron clothes, fabrics, etc.

ex hort′ (ĕg zôrt′), to incite or urge to good deeds.

priv′i lege (-lĕj), a special advantage or right.

clev′er, mentally keen; dexterous.

em bod′i ment, state of being embodied or incorporated.

col lapse′, an abrupt falling together; to break down.

is′sue (ĭsh′ū), the point in controversy; to send forth.

null, void; of no legal force.

im pul′sive, hasty; actuated by impulse.

un couth′ (-kōōth′), odd; ungainly; awkward.

im per′il, to put in danger or jeopardy.

har′ass, to annoy or vex; disturb.

man′u script, written or typewritten copy to be printed.

le′gion (-jŭn), an army; a multitude.

du′bi ous, doubtful; uncertain.

laun′dry, room or establishment where laundering is done.

ex tinct′, no longer living or active; extinguished.

pol′ish, to make smooth by rubbing; to make refined.

fal′ter (fôl′-), to show moral or physical hesitancy; to hesitate.

crea′ture, a living created being.

en grave′, to cut with an engraving tool.

in sip′id, without savor; tasteless; lacking in animation.

pre side′ (-zīd′), to act as chairman of a meeting.

re nounce′, to give up formally.

an′nu al, happening every year; yearly; lasting only one year.

O′ri ent, the countries collectively that are east of Europe.

tac′it (tăs′-), implied but not stated outright.

suf′frage, the right to vote.

in tact′, left complete or unimpaired.

re hearse′ (-hûrs′), to repeat; to drill in private.

sat′u rate, to fill with moisture; to soak.

ri′val, a competitor; an opponent.

em′a nate, to issue from a source; to originate.

cit′i zen, a native or naturalized inhabitant.

ko′dak, a portable camera.

ap pre′ci ate (-shĭ āt), to value justly; to rise in value.

LESSON 13

pro spec′tive, being still in the future; expected.

in′voice, a list showing the items and charges of merchandise.

glam′our (-ẽr), a deceptive spell or charm.

re strain′, to hold back; to check.

hy′drant, a discharge outlet from a water main.

vin′di cate, to defend successfully; to justify.

con′cert, a musical entertainment; concord.

re strict′, to limit; to confine.

re lease′ (-lēs′), to loosen; to liberate.

su preme′, highest in authority or power.

o pin′ion (-yŭn), what one thinks about any subject; judgment.

im pair′, to weaken; to injure.

in ure′ (ĭn ūr′), to accustom; to harden.

nine teenth′, the next after the eighteenth.

eth′ics, the science of morals.

sol′ace, comfort in grief or anxiety; relief.

vaude′ville (vōd′vĭl), a miscellaneous theatrical entertainment.

ten′et, a doctrine, opinion, or belief held as true.

par′lor, a reception room.

sal′a ry, a regular payment made for services; stipend.

her′i tage, that which is inherited; a birthright.

in clu′sive, including the things mentioned; comprising.

ru′mor (rōō′mẽr), a vague report; common talk.

sol′i ta ry, lonely; living alone.

con′se crate, to devote to a sacred purpose; sanctify.

e las′tic, springing back; having elasticity.

com mute′, to reduce to something less.

tran′script, a copy of a writing.

por′trait (pōr′-), a likeness of a person.

can′did, fully truthful; frank; sincere.

smug′gle, to import or export secretly without paying duty.

ad jure′, to entreat earnestly.

con sign′ (-sīn′), to ship to another to be sold.

cart′age, charge for carting; drayage.

for′ti eth, one of forty equal parts.

im mune′, exempt, as from disease; not liable to.

plat′en, the roller of a typewriter against which the type strikes.

her′ald, to announce publicly; to usher in; a messenger.

ad′age, a proverb; a maxim.

pro por′tion ate, being in due proportion; proportional.

LESSON 14

im per′a tive, urgent; not to be avoided or evaded.

thresh′old, a place or point of entrance; a doorsill.

ru′di ment (rōō′-), the first principle of any art or science.

di vulge′, to make known; disclose.

max′i mum, the greatest number, quantity, or degree possible.

ad verse, acting against; unfavorable; antagonistic.

vir′ile (vĭr′ĭl; vī′rĭl), masterful; manly; forceful.

pro hib′it, to forbid; to prevent.

ca reer′, one's accomplishments or general course of action.

so lic′it (-lĭs′-), to petition; to ask for with earnestness.

to′tal, the whole sum or amount; complete; to ascertain the sum.

at tack′, an assault; to assail.

mar′tyr, a sufferer for principle or opinion.

nui′sance (nū′-), anything offensive, annoying, or noxious.

plat, a plot of ground; a map or chart; to lay out.

per chance′, perhaps; possible.

sub′urbs, outlying parts of a city or of a town.

re peat′ed ly, again and again.

lau′rels, honors; distinction.

cyn′ic (sĭn′ĭk), one who thinks others always act from selfish motives; a sneering person.

char′ac ter, distinguishing qualities; a mark or symbol.

re spec′tive, relating to particular things; several.

in trigue′ (-trēg′), to plot or to scheme; a secret plot.

re li′ance, confidence; dependence.

pen′cil, an instrument useful for writing; to draw or write.

pan′el, a distinct section of wall, door, etc.; a jury list.

es pouse′ (-pouz′), to adopt; to advocate or defend.

di vest′, to deprive; to unclothe.

ten′or, high male voice; course; general tendency.

ex′qui site (ĕks′kwĭ zĭt), of surpassing quality or beauty.

par′ish, a religious society and territory where the members live.

lit′er al, word for word; exact.

bus′y, earnestly at work; industrious; diligent.

bo nan′za, a rich mine; anything that yields a large income.

fur′ni ture, household goods or furnishings.

wreck′age, remains of a wreck.

sem′blance, likeness; outward appearance; pretense.

sen′ti nel, a guard or watchman.

bas′ic (bās′-), fundamental; basal.

res′er voir (rĕz′ẽr vwôr), a place where anything, especially water, is stored up for use.

LESSON 15

sep′a rate, not united; distinct; to set apart from others.

di lem′ma, an embarrassing situation; a predicament.

bal′lot, a ticket for voting; act of voting.

ed′i fice, an imposing building.

cor′dial (-jăl), hearty; sincere; warm; that which exhilarates.

ap pli′ance, something used as a means to an end; a device.

op por tu′ni ty, a favorable occasion or chance.

brev′i ty, conciseness; shortness.

dil′a to ry, tending to cause delay; tardy.

mem o ran′dum, a brief note or informal record.

par′al lel, everywhere equidistant; similar.

en deav′or, to try earnestly.

con cil′i ate, to win over; to appease.

di verge′, to change in direction; to deviate.

un til′, up to; to the time when; till.

cap′tion, a title or heading.

be hoove′, to be necessary; incumbent.

ar′du ous, difficult; laborious.

prod′i gal, lavish; a spendthrift.

sup′ple ment, that which completes, adds to or corrects; to add something to.

busi′ness (bĭz′nĕs), occupation; mercantile transactions.

ver′dict, decision of a jury; any decision or conclusion.

vol′un ta ry, acting from choice; of one's own accord.

de fec′tive, deficient; imperfect.

mis cel la′ne ous, consisting of several kinds; variously mixed.

rec′ord, something written as evidence; a recorded achievement.

fu′gi tive, one fleeing from arrest or capture.

prof′it, gain or advantage.

em po′ri um, an important trading place.

for′tu nate, coming by good fortune; lucky.

fun da men′tal, pertaining to the foundation; basic.

ter′mi nate, to limit; to end.

av′a lanche, a sliding mass of snow, rocks, etc.

mit′i gate, to lessen or moderate; to alleviate.

stur′dy, having rugged health; strong.

de ci′sive, conclusive; positive.

mag a zine′, a storehouse; a periodical.

se′ri ous, earnest; not trifling.

e′dict, a public order or decree.

am a teur′ (-tûr′), one devoted to an act, sport, etc., for love of it and not as a profession.

Begin

LESSON 16

Monosyllables Often Misspelled

purge, to cleanse; to clear of guilt or liability.

crux (krŭks), the difficult or puzzling part of a question.

scene, a landscape; part of a play.

baize (bāz), a coarse woolen fabric used for table cloths, etc.

sluice (slōōs), an artificial channel for water; a floodgate.

urge, to press; to insist upon.

lurch, a sudden roll to one side; an embarrassing position.

gnash (năsh), to grind the teeth in anger or pain.

gist (jĭst), the main point; pith.

prone, prostrate; mentally disposed or inclined.

niche (nĭch), a hollow or recess, generally in a wall.

trite, commonplace; hackneyed.

aisle, a passsage between seats in a church or other building.

tithe, a tenth of one's income given to church or charity.

ruse (rōōz), a trick; an artifice.

feud (fūd), a persistent quarrel between families or clans.

cinch, a saddle girth; a sure or easy thing.

dirge, a funeral hymn or tune.

realm, a kingdom; empire; domain.

sponge (spŭnj), a marine animal and its fibrous skeleton; a parasite; to cleanse.

qualm, a feeling of sickness; a twinge of conscience.

lieu (lū), place; stead; used in the phrase *in lieu of*.

hence, for this reason; therefore.

tact, ability to deal with others without offending; address.

splurge (splûrj), a showy display; to make a great display.

thwart, to frustrate or defeat.

sketch, to outline; a rough outline; a short composition.

prove (prōōv), to demonstrate the truth of.

crude, raw; immature; uncultured.

gibe (jīb), to utter taunting, sarcastic words; to jeer.

quiz, to examine or coach by questions; to question closely.

source, the origin; fountainhead.

prude, one who makes an affected display of modesty.

scourge (skûrj), to afflict severely; a whip with thongs.

chute (shōōt), an inclined trough.

terse, elegantly concise; free of superfluous words; pithy.

slough (slŭf), to shed or cast off; to discard.

verge, the extreme edge; border.

sparse, thinly scattered; not dense.

mulch, any substance used to protect roots of plants; to cover with mulch.

LESSON 17
Monosyllables Often Misspelled

bloc (blŏk), a political group that votes and acts together.

myth (mĭth), a legend; an imaginary person, thing, or event.

spurn, to reject with contempt.

taunt, to reproach with sarcastic language; to jeer at.

kiln (kĭl), a heated chamber for burning, drying, or seasoning.

squelch, to crush; to silence.

shirk, to avoid or evade; one who evades a duty.

rouge (rōōzh), a cosmetic for coloring the cheeks or lips.

wrought (rôt), worked; not crude.

quay (kē), a pier; an artificial landing place.

chord (côrd), a harmonious combination of tones.

dearth, scarcity; lack; famine.

tryst (trĭst), a rendezvous or place of meeting.

crypt (krĭpt), a recess or vault, as under a church.

shrewd (shrōōd), keen; cunning.

plumb (plŭm), vertical; perpendicular.

cruise, to sail to and fro; a voyage at sea.

thyme (tīm), an aromatic herb.

wretch, a base or miserable person.

pledge (plĕj), a security for the performance of an act; to give a security or guarantee.

suave (swāv; swäv), pleasant in manner; gracious.

alms (ämz), anything given to relieve the poor; charity.

false, untrue; not well founded.

hoax, a mischievous deception or story; a practical joke.

flux (flŭks), a substance that promotes the fusion of metals.

wane, to grow less; to decrease.

font, an assortment of one size and style of type.

braze, to join with hard solder; to cover with brass.

franc (frănk), a French coin.

throe (thrō), a violent pain; extreme anguish or agony.

balm (bäm), anything that soothes pain or that heals.

staid, sedate; grave; steady.

bier (bēr), frame on which a corpse is placed.

swath (swôth), a line of grass cut by a scythe.

cleanse (klĕnz), to make clean.

taut (tôt), stretched; as, a *taut* rope.

vaunt, to brag; to boast; vain display.

sleuth (slōōth), a detective.

filch, to steal in a small way.

buoy (boi), a floating object moored to guide navigators; to support; to sustain.

LESSON 18
Monosyllables Often Misspelled

merge, to be absorbed into something else.

leech, one who clings to another to draw gain from him.

search, to go over or through and examine; act of searching.

sure (shōōr), certain; positive.

shale, a fragile rock resembling slate.

plunge (plŭnj), to rush into; any sudden or violent motion.

rue, to lament or be sorry for.

curt, concise and abrupt in act or expression.

grudge (grŭj), sullen malice or ill will; old cause of quarrel.

guest, a visitor; lodger; boarder.

duct, a tube or canal for conveying fluid.

route (rōōt), a way or road; to forward by a certain road.

mere, simple; absolute; only.

gaunt, emaciated, as with fasting; lean.

ledge (lĕj), a projecting ridge or edge; a shelf.

scrimp, to be sparing of; scanty.

knack (năk), quickness and cleverness in performance.

praise, to express approval; commendation.

salve (säv), a healing ointment.

leash (lēsh), a thong or cord by which a thing is held; to tie.

farce, something ridiculous; an absurd failure.

ream, a bundle of paper, usually 500 sheets; to enlarge.

slur, to pass over lightly; to slight; a disparaging remark.

ache (āk), a dull, continued pain.

seethe, to boil; to be in a state of boiling.

stanch (stånch), loyal; steadfast; zealous. Also, *staunch.*

lax, lacking firmness; negligent.

sheen, a glistening brightness; to shine or glisten.

suede (swād), a kind of leather, having an undressed surface.

faze, to disconcert; to worry; vex.

helm, the apparatus for steering a ship.

rout, to defeat disastrously; a disorderly flight.

lithe, bending easily; supple.

jute, a fiber used for bags, mats, twine, etc.

schism (sĭz'm), a division of a church into factions.

pert, forward; saucy; bold.

yacht (yŏt), a vessel built or fitted for pleasure.

sphinx (sfĭŋks), a symbol of silence and mystery.

psalm (säm), a sacred song or poem.

wreck (rĕk), the remains of anything ruined; to ruin or destroy.

LESSON 19
Analogous Words

su per sede', to supplant; to take the place of.

ex ceed', to go beyond the limit or measure of; to overdo.

pro ceed', to move forward.

suc ceed', to accomplish something attempted.

ac cede', to yield; to agree.

cede, to transfer; to give up.

con cede', to admit to be true; to yield.

in ter cede', to act between parties with a view to reconcile differences.

pre cede', to go before in time, rank, place, etc.

re cede', to fall back; to retreat.

se cede', to withdraw from fellowship, union or association.

ex pense', an outlay; a disbursement.

sus pense', a state of uncertainty or anxiety; suspension.

dis pense', to deal out in portions; to do without.

re sponse', to answer; responsive act or feeling.

in tense', extreme in degree.

im mense', very great or large.

con dense', to make more compact or dense; to concentrate.

li'cense, authority or permission to do something.

wel'come, to receive gladly; a cordial reception.

wel'fare, condition of health; happiness; prosperity.

al'most, nearly; well-nigh.

al read'y, prior to some specified time; previously.

al might'y, all-powerful.

al though (-thō), notwithstanding; though.

al to geth'er, without exception; wholly.

with al', likewise; at the same time.

tre men'dous, exceedingly great or large; dreadful.

stu pen'dous, wonderful; astonishing; amazing.

mo men'tous, very important.

pro mis'cu ous, confused; without order.

pre sump'tu ous (-zŭmp'-), bold and overconfident; arrogant.

sump'tu ous, luxurious; costly.

re pel', to drive back; to check the advance of.

pro pel', to drive onward by applied force.

ex cel', to go beyond or surpass.

im pel', to urge forward; to induce.

ex pel', to drive away; to eject.

com pel', to force to yield.

dis pel', to drive away by scattering; to banish.

See page 41 for words ending in *sede, ceed,* and *cede* arranged for visualization.

LESSON 20 (Oral)

Adjective, Adverb and Noun Suffixes

Al is an adjective suffix, meaning *belonging* or *pertaining to*; *ly* is an adverbial suffix, meaning *manner*; *ity* (sometimes *ty*) is a noun suffix, meaning *state* or *quality of being*.

Note—*Ly* is also sometimes an adjective suffix, as in *manly*.

roy'al	roy'al ly	roy'al ty
loy'al	loy'al ly	loy'al ty
cas'u al	cas'u al ly	cas'u al ty
in'ci dent	in ci den'tal	in ci den'tal ly
ac'ci dent	ac ci den'tal	ac ci den'tal ly
in ten'tion	in ten'tion al	in ten'tion al ly
ex cep'tion	ex cep'tion al	ex cep'tion al ly
con'fi dent	con'fi dent ly	con'fi dence
ev'i dent	ev'i dent ly	ev'i dence
a bun'dant	a bun'dant ly	a bun'dance
e vent'*	e ven'tu al	e ven'tu al ly
oc ca'sion	oc ca'sion al	oc ca'sion al ly
sim'i lar	sim'i lar ly	sim i lar'i ty
the'o ry	the o ret'i cal	the o ret'i cal ly
prin'ci pal	prin'ci pal ly	prin ci pal'i ty
punc'tu al	punc'tu al ly	punc tu al'i ty
vir'tue	vir'tu al	vir'tu al ly
con tin'ue	con tin'u al	con tin'u al ly
hab'it	ha bit'u al	ha bit'u al ly
me chan'ic	me chan'i cal	me chan'i cal ly
pe'ri od	pe ri od'i cal	pe ri od'i cal ly
meth'od	me thod'i cal	me thod'i cal ly
scarce	scarce'ly	scar'ci ty
se vere'	se vere'ly	se ver'i ty
sin cere'	sin cere'ly	sin cer'i ty

*Note 1—Sometimes a word is slightly modified before adding *al*.

Note 2—Observe that the words *surety*, *nicety*, and *entirety* take the suffix *ty* instead of *ity*, and, therefore, retain the *e* in accordance with rule 2, page 25.

Note 3—A few words ending in *ic* may be used as adjectives, either with or without the suffix *al*; as, *electric* or *electrical*; *geographic* or *geographical*. The corresponding adverbs, however, end in *ally*.

LESSON 21

The Law of Association

In the spelling of many troublesome words, the only difficulty hinges on one letter. In most of these words, the doubtful letter can be determined by associating the word with some other form of the word. Thus, by associating *preparation* with *prepare*, the obscure vowel *a* is made clear.

Teacher: Pronounce the first word of each pair.

ben'e fit	mi li'tia	fu'tile	mal'ice
be nef'i cent	mil'i ta ry	fu til'i ty	ma li'cious
val'id	hos'tile	no'ta ry	cha'os
va lid'i ty	hos til'i ty	no ta'ri al	cha ot'ic
fer'tile	fa'tal	rap'id	mir'a cle
fer til'i ty	fa tal'i ty	ra pid'i ty	mi rac'u lous
ag'ile	stu'pid	hos'pi tal	pri'or
a gil'i ty	stu pid'i ty	hos pi tal'i ty	pri or'i ty
fru'gal	mo'bile	mu nic'i pal	or'i gin
fru gal'i ty	mo bil'i ty	mu nic i pal'i ty	o rig'i nal
vi'tal	for'mal	sig'ni fy	im pede'
vi tal'i ty	for mal'i ty	sig nif'i cant	im ped'i ment
ex pense'	men'tal	di min'ish	gram'mar
ex pen'sive	men tal'i ty	dim i nu'tion	gram mat'i cal
de fense'	bru'tal	col'umn	friv'o lous
de fen'sive	bru tal'i ty	co lum'nar	fri vol'i ty
of fense'	sym'me try	vol'ume	me trop'o lis
of fen'sive	sym met'ri cal	vo lu'mi nous	met ro pol'i tan
sus pense'	va'ri ance	mag'ni fy	cus'to dy
sus pen'sion	va ri a'tion	mag nif'i cent	cus to'di an

Frugal, economical, saving; *frugality*, state or quality of being frugal; *valid*, sound, just, lawful; *agile* (ăj'ĭl), active, nimble; *formal*, in accordance with established form, stiff; *symmetry*, harmonious relation of parts; *futile*, useless, vain; *notary*, an officer who attests writings, etc.; *municipal*, pertaining to a city or town; *malice*, spite, ill will; *chaos* (kā'ŏs), utter disorder or confusion; *miracle*, a wonderful thing, a marvel; *impede*, to obstruct, hinder; *custody*, a keeping or guarding.

LESSON 22

The Law of Association

Note—Observe that in some pairs of words the obscure vowel in the first word can be easily determined by associating the first word with the second. Thus, the obscure vowel *e* in *academy* is made plain by associating *academy* with *academic*, and the obscure vowel *a* in the second syllable of *academic* is made plain by associating *academic* with *academy*.

Teacher: Pronounce the second word of each pair.

fac′ile	cer′tain	a cad′e my	ex pire′
fa cil′i ty	as cer tain′	ac a dem′ic	ex pi ra′tion
fi′nite	strict	dip′lo mat	in spire′
def′i nite	strict′ly	di plo′ma cy	in spi ra′tion
com pile′	mag net′ic	se′cret	per spire′
com pi la′tion	mag′net ism	sec′re ta ry	per spi ra′tion
mi′nor	de clare′	oc cu pa′tion	as pire′
mi nor′i ty	dec la ra′tion	oc′cu pan cy	as pi ra′tion
com plete′	de grade′	con tin u a′tion	sta′tion er
com′ple ment	deg ra da′tion	con tin′u ance	sta′tion er y
con duce′	pre pare′	pres er va′tion	con fec′tion er
con du′cive	prep a ra′tion	pre serv′a tive	con fec′tion er y
ra′di ate	ex pla na′tion	con ver sa′tion	syn′o nym
ra′di ant	ex plan′a to ry	con′ver sant	syn on′y mous
hes′i tate	ob ser va′tion	stim′u late	con ser va′tion
hes′i tan cy	ob serv′a to ry	stim′u lant	con serv′ a tive
no to′ri ous	com pete′	med′i cine	rid′i cule
no to ri′e ty	com pet′i tor	me dic′i nal	ri dic′u lous
mon′ey	er′ror	am big′u ous	re cip′ro cate
mon′e ta ry	er ro′ne ous	am bi gu′i ty	rec i proc′i ty

Facile (făs′ĭl), easily done, not difficult; *finite*, having bounds or limits; *compile*, to put together extracts; *minor*, under age, of little importance; *conducive*, contributing to a result, helping; *radiate*, to send out in rays, as light or heat; *monetary*, pertaining to money; *diplomacy*, tact, shrewdness, skill; *preservative*, that which tends to preserve; *conversant*, fully informed; *ambiguous*, doubtful, uncertain as to meaning; *synonymous*, similar in meaning; *reciprocate*, to give and return mutually.

LESSON 23

Words Having Internal Changes

The primitive form of most words, on taking a suffix, remains unchanged, or only the final letter is changed or dropped. There are, however, a few words, most of which are contained in this lesson, in which a change is made in the body of the word on taking a suffix.

Note—Words ending in *c* take the letter *k* before a suffix beginning with *e, i* or *y*, so that the *c* may not be pronounced like *s*.

Teacher: Pronounce the second word of each pair.

main tain'	en'ter	lease	trag'ic
main'te nance	en'trance	les see'	trag'e dy
sus tain'	re mem'ber	cease	stra te'gic
sus'te nance	re mem'brance	ces sa'tion	strat'a gem
ab stain'	en cum'ber	re peat'	o'men
ab'sti nence	en cum'brance	rep e ti'tion	om'i nous
per tain'	hin'der	pro ceed'	fire
per'ti nent	hin'drance	pro ce'dure	fier'y
de claim'	dis as'ter	dis creet'	pan'ic
dec la ma'tion	dis as'trous	dis cre'tion	pan'ick y
ex plain'	won'der	re pair'	frol'ic
ex pla na'tion	won'drous	rep a ra'tion	frol'ick ing
pro claim'	lus'ter	pre vail'	mim'ic
proc la ma'tion	lus'trous	prev'a lent	mim'icked
re claim'	stu'pid	com par'i son	pic'nic
rec la ma'tion	stu'pe fy	com par'a tive	pic'nick er
ex claim'	liq'uid	mys te'ri ous	rol'lic
ex cla ma'tion	liq'ue fy	mys'ti fy	rol'lick ing

Note—*Hin'der ance* is also good usage.

Reclamation, the act of recovering or restoring; *sustain,* to hold up, to support, to bear up under; *sustenance,* act of maintaining, that which supports life; *maintenance,* the act of supporting, defending; *encumber,* to place a burden on, as a debt or legal claim; *prevalent,* common, widespread; *reparation,* the act of restoring to good condition, indemnity; *comparative,* estimated by comparison.

LESSON 24

Silent *e* Dropped

Rule 1—Words ending in silent *e* drop the *e* before a suffix beginning with a vowel, except words ending in *ce* or *ge* followed by *able* or *ous*.

Key Word: use—using, usable, usage.

Note 1—Since *c* and *g* always have the hard sound before *a* and *o*, words ending in *ce* or *ge* retain final *e* before the suffix *able* or *ous* in order to preserve the soft sound of *c* and *g*; as, *change, changeable; peace, peaceable; advantage, advantageous.*

Teacher: Select forty words from the second and third columns and from the words in the notes.

move	mov′ing	mov′a ble
de sire′	de sir′ing	de sir′ous
as sure′	as sur′ing	as sur′ance
ad vise′	ad vis′ing	ad vis′a ble
no′tice	no′tic ing	no′tice a ble
charge	charg′ing	charge′a ble
man′age	man′ag ing	man′age able
di vine′	di vine′ly	di vin′i ty
trace	trac′ing	trace′a ble
in sure′	in sur′ing	in sur′ance
val′ue	val′u ing	val′u a ble
ob scure′	ob scur′ing	ob scu′ri ty
ad mire′	ad mir′ing	ad′mi ra ble
ex cuse′	ex cus′ing	ex cus′a ble
ar rive′	ar riv′ing	ar riv′al
ap prove′	ap prov′ing	ap prov′al
ex cite′	ex cit′ing	ex cit′a ble
re verse′	re vers′ing	re vers′i ble
se cure′	se cur′ing	se cu′ri ty

Note 2—Observe that words ending in *ie* drop the *e* and change the *i* to *y* when adding *ing*, so as to prevent two *i*'s from coming together; as, *die, dying; lie, lying; tie, tying; vie, vying.*

Note 3—Observe also that the *e* is retained in *hoeing, shoeing, toeing,* and *canoeing* to avoid forming the diphthong *oi*. The *e* is also retained in the words *dyeing, tingeing,* and *singeing* to distinguish these words from *dying, singing,* and *tinging.* The word *mileage* is preferably spelled with the *e*.

LESSON 25

Silent *e* Retained

Rule 2—Words ending in silent *e* retain the *e* before a suffix beginning with a consonant.

Key Word: **use—useful, useless.**

Note—Observe that the spelling of the words in this lesson are governed by Rules 1 and 2.

Teacher: Select forty words from the second and third columns and from the exceptions.

ad vance′	ad vanc′ing	ad vance′ment
strange	strange′ly	strange′ness
de base′	de bas′ing	de base′ment
ac crue′	ac cru′ing	ac cru′al
re tire′	re tir′ing	re tire′ment
shape	shape′ly	shap′ing
pur′sue	pur su′ing	pur su′ance
waste	waste′ful *	wast′ing
an nounce′	an nounc′ing	an nounce′ment
hope	hop′ing	hope′less
en large′	en larg′ing	en large′ment
state	stat′ing	state′ment
blame	blame′less	blam′ing
a bate′	a bate′ment	a bat′able
a muse′	a mus′ing	a muse′ment
rare	rare′ly	rar′i ty
change	change′less	chang′ing
es cape′	es cap′ing	es cape′ment
in duce	in duc′ing	in duce′ment
force	force′ful	forc′ing

Exceptions:

judg′ment	abridg′ment	tru ly
ac knowl′edg ment	ar′gu ment	whol ly
lodg′ment	du′ly	aw′ful

Note—*Judgement, lodgement, acknowledgement,* and *abridgement* are sanctioned.

* Note—Observe that *ful,* as a suffix, is spelled with one *l.*

Chronos - name of father time

LESSON 26

Words in which **ph = f, gh = f, ch = k,** and **i = y.**

al'ien (āl'yĕn), a foreigner; wholly different in nature.

bril'liant (-yănt), sparkling; shining.

a mel'io rate (*à* mēl'yŏ rāt), to make better.

ca tas'tro phe (-fē), a calamity.

ar'chi tect (-kĭ-), one who plans buildings.

at'mos phere (-fēr-), the air surrounding the earth.

chlo'ro form, an anaesthetic.

al'pha bet, the letters of a language in their usual order.

chris'ten (krĭs''n), to baptize; to give a Christian name.

chron'ic, continuous; constant.

ech'o (ĕk'ō), reflected sound.

de ci'pher (dĕ sī'fēr), to translate; to make out.

em'pha sis (-fà-), stress; force.

ep'och (ĕp'ŏk), an important period of history.

hy'phen (-fĕn), a mark used to join words or separate syllables.

mel'an chol y (-kŏl-), despondency.

neph'ew (nĕf'ū), the son of a brother or sister.

or'ches tra (-kĕs trà), a band of musicians.

or'phan (-făn), a child deprived of its parents by death.

con ven'ience (-yĕns), that which promotes comfort or advantage.

pam'phlet (-flĕt), a small unbound book.

phan'tom (-tŭm), an apparition.

pa ro'chi al (pà rō'kĭ ăl), pertaining to a parish.

phar'ma cy (fär'-), a drug store.

par'a graph (-gràf), a division of a discourse.

phase (fāz), one side or view of a subject.

phe nom'e nal (fē-), remarkable.

pho'no graph, an instrument for reproducing music, etc.

phos'phate (fŏs'fāt), a salt of phosphoric acid.

pin'ion (-yŭn), a cogwheel.

sched'ule, a list; time-table.

scheme (skēm), a systematic plan; to plot.

pe cul'iar (-yàr), strange; odd.

si'phon (sī'fŏn), a bent tube for drawing off liquids.

sphere (sfēr), a globe; range of action, influence, etc.

tri'umph, a conquest or victory.

fa mil'iar (-yàr), closely acquainted; intimate.

val'iant (-yănt), courageous; brave; heroic.

proph'et, one who delivers divine messages or foretells the future.

ar'chives (-kīvz), place where public records are kept.

LESSON 27

Unusual Combinations of Letters

In certain words *gue* has the sound of hard *g; que* has the sound of *k; rh* and *rrh* have the sound of *r*.

tech nique' (tĕk nēk'), technical skill; style of performance.

fa tigue' (-tēg'), exhaustion of strength by toil; weariness.

phy sique' (fĭ zēk'), physical appearance.

brogue (brōg), a peculiar dialect.

vague, not clearly stated or understood; indefinite; hazy.

cat'a logue,* a list of titles or articles; to put in a list.

plaque (plȧk), a thin piece of decorated metal or earthen ware.

ob lique' (-lēk'), not upright.

rheu mat'ic (rōō-), pertaining to, or affected with, rheumatism.

tongue, the organ of speech and taste; a language.

mon'o logue* (-lŏg), a dramatic part for a single performer.

an tique' (-tēk'), ancient; a relic.

dem'a gogue* (-gŏg), an insincere political leader.

rhythm (rĭth'm), regular succession of motions, sounds, etc.

ped'a gogue,* a schoolmaster.

plague, to vex or annoy; a pestilence.

trav'e logue,* a lecture on travel, usually with illustrations.

o paque' (ŏ pāk'), not transparent; not admitting passage to light.

dec'a logue* (-lŏg), The Ten Commandments.

brusque (brŭsk), rude; curt; blunt.

ar a besque' (-bĕsk'), a kind of fanciful ornamentation.

bur lesque' (-lĕsk'), a ridiculous representation; a travesty.

di'a logue* (-lŏg), a conversation between two or more persons.

rogue (rōg), a dishonest person.

myrrh (mûr), an aromatic gum obtained from an Oriental shrub.

clique (klēk), a small, exclusive social set; a ring.

syn'a gogue,* a building or place for religious worship.

gro tesque' (-tĕsk'), oddly formed.

ca tarrh' (-tär'), inflammation of a mucous membrane.

toque (tōk), a woman's close-fitting hat with no brim.

vogue, fashion; mode of usage.

mosque (mŏsk), a Mohammedan temple of worship.

* Webster sanctions *catalog, travelog,* and *dialog,* while the Standard Dictionary prefers dropping *ue* from all these words.

In the following words and a few others, *u* after *g* has the sound of *w,* just as it always has after *q*. Consult the dictionary for definition.

extinguish	**anguish**	**language**	**sanguine**
distinguish	**languid**	**languish**	**linguist**

LESSON 28

Final Consonant Doubled

Rule 3—Monosyllables and words of more than one syllable accented on the last syllable, ending in a single consonant, preceded by a single vowel, double the final consonant on taking a suffix beginning with a vowel.

The Four Conditions
1. The word must be accented on the last syllable.
2. It must end in a single consonant.
3. Final consonant must be preceded by a single vowel.
4. The suffix must begin with a vowel.

Key Word: **remit—remitted, remitting, remittance**

Note—When the accent is thrown back on the first syllable in the derivative, the consonant is not doubled; as, *pref' er ence, def' er ence.*

Teacher: Select forty words from the second, third and fourth columns, and from the exceptions.

plan	planned	plan'ning	plan'ner
ship	shipped	ship'ping	ship'per
beg	begged	beg'ging	beg'gar
blot	blot'ted	blot'ting	blot'ter
con trol'	con trolled'	con trol'ling	con trol'ler
pro pel'	pro pelled'	pro pel'ling	pro pel'ler
ad mit'	ad mit'ted	ad mit'ting	ad mit'tance
trans mit'	trans mit'ted	trans mit'ting	trans mit'ter
ac quit'*	ac quit'ted	ac quit'ting	ac quit'tal
con cur'	con curred'	con cur'ring	con cur'rence
oc cur'	oc curred'	oc cur'ring	oc cur'rence
re cur'	re curred'	re cur'ring	re cur'rence
re fer'	re ferred'	re fer'ring	ref'er ence
pre fer'	pre ferred'	pre fer'ring	pref'er ence
de fer'	de ferred'	de fer'ring	def'er ence
con fer'	con ferred'	con fer'ring	con'fer ence
in fer'	in ferred'	in fer'ring	in'fer ence

Exceptions:

trans fer', trans fer'a ble; crys'tal, crys'tal lize; hum'bug, hum'-bugged, hum'bug ging; hand'i cap, hand'i capped, hand'i cap ping; cha grin', cha grined', cha grin'ing; ex cel', ex'cel lent, ex'cel lence, ex'-cel len cy.

* Note—Words in which the final consonant is preceded by *qu* followed by a single vowel come under this rule, since *qu* is equivalent to *kw.*

LESSON 29

Final Consonant Not Doubled

Caution—Words not accented on the last syllable, words ending in more than one consonant, and words in which the final consonant is preceded by more than one vowel do not double the final consonant on taking a suffix beginning with a vowel.

Note 1—While the derivatives of *kidnap* and *worship* are preferably spelled with one *p*, they may be spelled with two *p*'s.

Note 2—*Cancellation*, though derived from a word not accented on the last syllable, is spelled only with two *l*'s by Webster.

Teacher: Select forty words from the second, third and fourth columns.

wor'ship	wor'shiped	wor'ship ing	wor'ship er
kid'nap	kid'naped	kid'nap ing	kid'nap er
lim'it	lim'it ed	lim'it ing	lim'i ta tion
dif'fer	dif'fered	dif'fer ing	dif'fer ence
ap pear'	ap peared'	ap pear' ing	ap pear'ance
cur tail'	cur tailed'	cur tail'ing	cur tail'er
dream	dreamed	dream'ing	dream'er
load	load'ed	load'ing	load'er
dine	dined	din'ing	din'er
trav'el*	trav'eled	trav'el ing	trav'el er
mar'vel	mar'veled	mar'vel ing	mar'vel ous
coun'sel	coun'seled	coun'sel ing	coun'sel or
rev'el	rev'eled	rev'el ing	rev'el er
e'qual	e'qualed	e'qual ing	e qual'i ty
la'bel	la'beled	la'bel ing	la'bel er
mod'el	mod'eled	mod'el ing	mod'el er
tun'nel	tun'neled	tun'nel ing	tun'nel er
jew'el	jew'eled	jew'el ing	jew'el er
can'cel	can'celed	can'cel ing	can'cel er
quar'rel	quar'reled	quar'rel ing	quar'rel er
lev'el	lev'eled	lev'el ing	lev'el er

Note 3—Verbs ending in *l* preceded by a single vowel, though not accented on the last syllable, are, by some authorities, spelled with two *l*'s on taking a suffix beginning with a vowel, but the preference should be given to one *l*.

LESSON 30
Words Ending in *ous* and *us*

Ous is an adjective suffix, meaning *full of, abounding in, of the nature of, having the qualities of, like.* Adjectives ending in *ous* are usually derived from nouns.

Principle—Adjectives, except *bogus* and *minus*, end in *ous;* as, *pomp, pompous.* Nouns end in *us;* as, *campus.* Both terminations are pronounced *ŭs.*

ap pa ra'tus, things provided as a means to an end.

vil'lain ous, wicked; evil; depraved.

di ver'si ty, difference; variety.

per'il ous, hazardous; dangerous.

viv'id, bright; clear; striking.

qui e'tus, that which quiets or calms.

flag'rant, openly wicked; heinous.

mis'chiev ous, inclined to mischief.

rel'ic, a remnant of what has passed away.

pac'i fy, to make peaceful; to calm.

vig'or ous, strong; robust; lusty.

im'pe tus, momentum; impulse.

pen'al ty, the punishment fixed for a crime or offense.

hu'mor ous, amusing; comical; droll.

in cip'i ent, beginning; pertaining to the first stages.

cau'cus, a political meeting.

par'a site, an organism living on another; a hanger-on.

har mo'ni ous, peaceful; symmetrical.

nu'cle us, a center of development; central mass; kernel.

va'ri ous, different; many-sided.

cen'sus, an official numbering of the population.

nerv'ous, easily agitated or excited.

pan a ce'a, a universal remedy.

ig no ra'mus, an ignorant person.

lu'cra tive, highly profitable.

cour'te ous, showing courtesy; polite.

re tort', a sharp or witty reply.

stim'u lus, a goad; an incentive.

pen'ni less, without a penny; destitute.

seg'ment, a section; part set off.

po'rous, full of small openings.

ter'mi nus, the end; terminal.

re lin'quish, to give up; to renounce claim to.

gen'ius, a person of high mental superiority.

cul'mi nate, to attain the highest point or degree.

pre'vi ous, going before; prior.

pre cip'i tate, to throw headlong; to hasten.

bo'nus, a premium; an extra allowance.

e nor'mous, greatly exceeding the usual size; immense.

sta'tus, state; condition; rank.

LESSON 31
Words Ending in *cal* and *cle*

Principle—*Cal* is an adjective termination; *cle* is a noun termination.

Note 1—*Radical*, *periodical*, and *rascal*, though used as either adjectives or nouns, end in *cal*.

Note 2—Observe that the ending *cal* is always preceded by the *i* vowel, with the exception of *reciprocal*.

spec′ta cle, a noteworthy sight; a device to aid the sight.

re cip′ro cal, alternating; mutually interchangeable.

rep′ri mand, to reprove formally.

re cep′ta cle, that which receives and contains something.

par tic′u lar, fastidious; special.

skep′ti cal, unbelieving; doubting.

dig′ni fy, to exalt; to honor.

ve′hi cle, a kind of conveyance.

clas′si cal, pertaining to the first rank in literature or art.

pin′na cle, the highest point.

spin′dle, a slender pin or rod.

sur′gi cal, pertaining to surgery.

pre par′a to ry, serving to fit for something further.

bar′na cle, a shellfish that clings to rocks, ships, etc.

be speak′, to ask for in advance.

ar′ti cle, a particular thing; an essay.

ju′bi lant, exultingly glad.

hur′ried ly, hastily; speedily.

typ′i cal, like others of its kind; characteristic.

for′ti tude, firmness in confronting danger or trouble.

tech′ni cal, pertaining to some art, science, trade, etc.

par′ti cle, a minute portion of matter; small amount.

a ban′don, to give up; to forsake.

me chan′i cal, pertaining to machinery or mechanism.

pu′ri fy, to make pure; cleanse.

cler′i cal, relating to a clerk.

de crep′it, infirm; worn out.

i den′ti cal, precisely the same.

cu ri os′i ty, something strange or rare; inquisitiveness.

ver′ti cal, upright; perpendicular.

in im′i cal, hostile; antagonistic.

ob′sta cle, an obstruction; barrier.

ep i dem′ic, widespread; a widely prevalent disease.

prac′ti cal, opposed to theoretical; useful.

ninth, next after the eighth.

con tam′i nate, to make impure; to pollute.

a bol′ish, to do away with.

prim′i tive, original; simple.

eth′i cal, pertaining to right and wrong conduct.

vict′uals (vit′lz), prepared food for human beings; viands.

LESSON 32

Adjectives Ending in *able* and *ible*

Principle 1—If there is a corresponding noun ending in *tion* preceded by *a*, the adjective ends in *able*.

Key Words:
    com men da′tion   **ac cep ta′tion**
    com mend′a ble   **ac cept′a ble**

Principle 2—If there is a corresponding noun ending in *tion* or *sion* not preceded by *a*, the adjective ends in *ible*.

Key Words:
    per mis′sion   **col lec′tion**
    per mis′si ble   **col lect′i ble**

Teacher: Pronounce the second word of each pair.

du ra′tion	ir ri ta′tion	vi′sion	sub mer′sion
du′ra ble	ir′ri ta ble	vis′i ble	sub mers′i ble
rep u ta′tion	ap pre′ci a tion	ad mis′sion	di ges′tion
rep′u ta ble	ap pre′ci a ble	ad mis′si ble	di gest′i ble
va ri a′tion	pen e tra′tion	ac ces′sion	col lap′sion
va′ri a ble	pen′e tra ble	ac ces′si ble	col laps′i ble
ad mi ra′tion	es ti ma′tion	di vi′sion	com pres′sion
ad′mi ra ble	es′ti ma ble	di vis′i ble	com press′i ble
con so la′tion	in flam ma′tion	re ver′sion	de struc′tion
con sol′a ble	in flam′ma ble	re vers′i ble	de struct′i ble
pres en ta′tion	dis pen sa′tion	re duc′tion	per fec′tion
pre sent′a ble	in dis pen′sa ble	re duc′i ble	per fect′i ble
ad o ra′tion	tol′er a tion	rep re hen′sion	in ver′sion
a dor′a ble	in tol′er a ble	rep re hen′si ble	in vert′i ble
a bom i na′tion	rec on cil i a′tion	com bus′tion	com pre hen′sion
a bom′i na ble	ir rec on cil′a ble	com bus′ti ble	com pre hen′si ble

A Special Group

With the exception of *perceptible*, *susceptible*, and *corruptible*, words having nouns ending in *ption* or *sition* form the adjective by adding *able* to the root word.

re ceive′	re cep′tion	re ceiv′a ble
con ceive′	con cep′tion	con ceiv′a ble
per ceive′	per cep′tion	per ceiv′a ble
pre sume′	pre sump′tion	pre sum′a ble
re deem′	re demp′tion	re deem′a ble
sup pose′	sup po si′tion	sup pos′a ble

LESSON 33
Adjectives Ending in *able* and *ible*

Principle 3—If there is no corresponding noun ending in *tion* or *sion*, the adjective ends in *able* if the suffix can be dropped and still leave a complete word.

Key Words: **pass**   **avail'**
pass'a ble   **a vail'a ble**

Principle 4—If there is no corresponding noun ending in *tion* or *sion*, the adjective ends in *ible* if the suffix cannot be dropped and leave a complete word.

Key Words: **fea'si ble**   **cred'i ble**

Teacher: Select forty words from the second and third columns and from the exceptions.

de bate'	de bat'a ble	au'di ble
ad just'	ad just'a ble	leg'i ble
a gree'	a gree'a ble	tan'gi ble
a void'	a void'a ble	cru'ci ble
ac count'	ac count'a ble	ter'ri ble
pre fer'	pref'er a ble	el'i gi ble
de pend'	de pend'a ble	plau'si ble
be lieve'	be liev'a ble	in del'i ble
de mount'	de mount'a ble	com pat'i ble
re gret'	re gret'ta ble	in flex'i ble
com'fort	com'fort a ble	in fal'li ble
com pare'	com'pa ra ble	in vin'ci ble
a dapt'	a dapt'a ble	neg'li gi ble
con trol'	con trol'la ble	sus cep'ti ble
at tain'	at tain'a ble	in cor'ri gi ble
eq'ui ty	eq'ui ta ble	in tel'li gi ble
char'i ty	char'i ta ble	flex'i ble
mis take'	un mis tak'a ble	gul'li ble
ques'tion *	ques'tion a ble	hor'ri ble

* Note 1—If the suffix is added to a word ending in *tion*, *able* is required.

The following words are exceptions to the principles governing *able* and *ible* and must, therefore, be memorized individually:

for'ci ble	af'fa ble	hos'pi ta ble
dis cern'i ble	ten'a ble	for'mi da ble
con tempt'i ble	pal'pa ble	in ev'i ta ble
ir re sist'i ble	a me'na ble	in ex'o ra ble

LESSON 34

Words Ending in *ize, ise,* and *yze*

Principle—With few exceptions, when the word is derived from some other word, the ending is *ize;* when it is not derived from some other word, the ending is *ise;* as, *item, itemize; colony, colonize; exercise.*

Note—Observe that *analyze* and *paralyze* end in *yze;* and that *capsize, prize, size, baptize, ostracize* are not spelled in accordance with the principle.

Teacher: Select forty words from the second and third columns and from the illustrations and exceptions.

pa′tron	pat′ron ize	re vise′
vis′u al	vis′u al ize	de vise′
au′thor	au′thor ize	de spise′
i tal′ic	i tal′i cize	de mise′
mag′net	mag′net ize	sur mise′
sub′si dy	sub′si dize	ap prise′
mem′o ry	mem′o rize	sur prise′
sum′ma ry	sum′ma rize	com prise′
jour′nal	jour′nal ize	dis guise′
stand′ard	stand′ard ize	ap praise′
a pol′o gy	a pol′o gize	chas tise′
cap′i tal	cap′i tal ize	ex′er cise
har′mo ny	har′mo nize	par′a dise
gen′er al	gen′er al ize	fran′chise
jeop′ard y	jeop′ard ize	su per vise′
scru′ti ny	scru′ti nize	com′pro mise
cir′cu lar	cir′cu lar ize	en′ter prise
mo nop′o ly	mo nop′o lize	mer′chan dise
sym′pa thy	sym′pa thize	en fran′chise
min′i mum	min′i mize	ad′ver tise

Visualize, to form a mental picture; *subsidize,* to aid, as a private enterprise, with public money; *summarize,* to state briefly or concisely; *scrutinize,* to examine closely; *monopolize,* to acquire the exclusive possession or control of anything; *minimize,* to reduce to the smallest possible amount or degree; *demise,* death, to convey property by will or lease; *surmise,* to infer on slight grounds; *apprise,* to inform, to acquaint; *chastise,* to punish; *franchise,* a right or privilege.

LESSON 35

Words Ending in *or* and *er*

When used as noun suffixes *or* and *er* usually mean *one who* or *that which*. In nearly all words *or* is pronounced like *er*.

Principle 1—Words of more than one syllable ending in *ate* take the suffix *or*.

Principle 2—Words ending in *ss*, *ct*, or *vey*, with few exceptions, take the ending *or*. Most other words take the ending *er*.

Note—Observe that the suffix *or* carries with it the final letter of the root word and that the suffix *er* does not.

el'e vate	el'e va tor	con fess'	con fes'sor
cul'ti vate	cul'ti va tor	com press'	com pres'sor
e lim'i nate	e lim'i na tor	trans gress'	trans gres'sor
e vap'o rate	e vap'o ra tor	con'tract	con trac'tor
lu'bri cate	lu'bri ca tor	in spect'	in spec'tor
per'fo rate	per'fo ra tor	ex tract'	ex trac'tor
in'sti gate	in'sti ga tor	con duct'	con duc'tor
leg'is late	leg'is la tor	sur vey'	sur vey'or
nu'mer ate	nu'mer a tor	con vey'	con vey'or
per'co late	per'co la tor	de sign'	de sign'er
ren'o vate	ren'o va tor	con sume'	con sum'er
ven'ti late	ven'ti la tor	ex am'ine	ex am'in er
im'i tate	im i ta'tor	im'port	im port'er
mod'er ate	mod'er a tor	con tain'	con tain'er
pre var'i cate	pre var'i ca tor	com'fort	com'fort er
re frig'er ate	re frig'er a tor	ad'ver tise	ad ver tis'er
ma nip'u late	ma nip'u la tor	sup port'	sup port'er
mu'ti late	mu ti la'tor	ad just'	ad just'er
cre ate'	cre a'tor	re port'	re port'er
o rig'i nate	o rig'i na tor	can'vass	can'vass er

Lubricate, to lessen friction by oil or the like; *perforate,* to pierce through; *instigate,* to stimulate to a bad action; *percolate,* to pass through fine openings, to strain; *renovate,* to renew, to clean; *prevaricate,* to deviate from the truth; *manipulate,* to manage artfully or fraudulently, to handle; *transgress,* to violate a rule or law, to sin; *survey,* to measure, as land, a comprehensive view; *design,* an outline, plan, or drawing; to plan or devise; *canvass,* to seek orders, support, votes, etc.

LESSON 36

Words Ending in *ant* and *ent*

Principle—*Ant* and *ent*, as adjective suffixes, mean *being* or *doing;* as noun suffixes, they mean *one who* or *that which*.

Note—Bear in mind that soft *c* and soft *g* are followed by *e*, as, in *innocent;* and that hard *c* and hard *g* are followed by *a;* as, in *vacant*.

con stit'u ent, one represented; a necessary part.

i tin'er ant, going from place to place.

in gre'di ent, a constituent part.

hur'ri cane, a gale of unusual violence.

sol'vent, able to pay all debts.

re cip'i ent, one who or that which receives.

ti'tle, a name; right to property.

con tin'gent, accidental; conditional.

mag nif'i cent, splendid; sublime.

i o'ta, a very small quantity or degree; particle.

vig'i lant, being on the alert.

ge'ni al, kindly and sympathetic.

pet'u lant, peevish; impatient.

do mes'tic, pertaining to the home; tame.

strin'gent, strict; exacting.

lunch'eon, light repast between meals.

op po'nent, one who opposes.

de file', to make foul; to corrupt.

ex po'nent, one who explains or interprets something.

ąp par'el, clothing; dress; garb.

ig'no rant, destitute of knowledge; uneducated.

prom'i nent, distinguished; conspicuous.

pur su'ant, in accordance with.

im'pli cate, to involve in a fault or crime.

el'e gant, luxurious; tasteful.

su per in tend'ent, an overseer; director.

ges'ture, bodily motion or posture.

dil'i gent, industrious; persevering; painstaking.

lux u'ri ant, vigorous in growth.

per'ish, to pass away or die; to be destroyed.

as sail'ant, one who attacks.

cri'sis, a critical moment.

o be'di ent, dutiful; submissive.

be lat'ed, delayed; overtaken by night.

re luc'tant, averse; unwilling.

en coun'ter, to contend with; a conflict.

ac quaint', to inform; to notify.

de face', to disfigure; to mar.

de pend'ent, one who depends on another; relying on some one.

in stead', in place of; in lieu.

LESSON 37

Words Ending in *ance, ancy, ence, ency*

Ance, ancy, ence, ency are noun suffixes, meaning *the act, state,* or *quality of.* They are usually derived from adjectives ending in *ant* or *ent;* as, *fragrant, fragrance; urgent, urgency.*

Note—Observe that words ending in *nt* drop the *t* before the noun suffix *cy;* as, *vacant, vacancy.*

mag nif'i cence, splendor; grandeur of appearance.

espe'cial, exceptional; noteworthy.

neg'li gence, carelessness; neglect.

ra'ti o (ra shǐ ō; rā' shō), relative rate; proportion.

co in'ci dence, accidental agreement.

re miss', careless; negligent.

dil'i gence, careful attention; industry.

le'ni en cy, mildness; forbearance.

au'tumn, third season of the year.

prom'i nence, conspicuousness.

sol'ven cy, state of being solvent.

con sist'en cy, harmony; firmness.

strin'gen cy, strictness; closeness.

eu'lo gy, high praise; commendation.

val'or, personal bravery; courage.

clear'ance, removal of an obstruction; act of clearing.

quan'ti ty, a large portion or mass.

or'gan ize, to bring into systematic coöperation.

con tin'gen cy, a chance or possible occurrence.

ret'i cence, inclination to keep silent; reserve in speech.

re luc'tance, unwillingness; disinclination.

dum'my, a sham or make-believe.

vig'i lance, watchfulness; caution.

ex alt' (ĕg zôlt'), to put in a high place; to glorify.

al low'ance, that which is allowed; share; portion.

ig'no rance, a lack of knowledge.

lux u'ri ance, a rank, vigorous growth.

pur su'ance, act of pursuing.

plas'tic, capable of being molded.

al li'ance, union of interests.

ec'sta sy, excessive joy; rapture.

dif'fi cult, hard to do; involved.

cur'so ry, superficial; hasty.

o be'di ence, submission to authority.

de pend'ence, reliance; trust.

pit'tance, a small portion, especially of money.

de spond'en cy, mental depression.

el'e gance, the state or quality of being elegant.

fluc'tu ate, rise and fall; to waver; to vacillate.

syn'di cate, an association or combination of financiers.

LESSON 38

Words Ending in *y*

Rule 4—Words ending in *y* preceded by a consonant change the *y* to *i* before any suffix except one beginning with *i*.

Note 1—When the suffix begins with *i*, the *y* is retained to prevent two *i*'s from coming together; as, *copy, copying, copyist; accompany, accompanying.*

Note 2—After *t* the *y* is usually changed to *e* before the suffix *ous* to *avoid* forming the syllable *tious* (shŭs); as *plenty, plenteous; bounty, bounteous.* In a few words *y* after *t* is dropped before the suffix *able* or *ous;* as, *charity, charitable; calamity, calamitous; iniquity, iniquitous.*

Teacher: Select forty words from the second, third and fourth columns.

no'ti fy	no'ti fy ing	no'ti fied	no ti fi ca'tion
mod'i fy	mod'i fy ing	mod'i fied	mod i fi ca'tion
spec'i fy	spec'i fy ing	spec'i fied	spec i fi ca'tion
jus'ti fy	jus'ti fy ing	jus'ti fied	jus ti fi ca'tion
rat'i fy	rat' i fy ing	rat'i fied	rat i fi ca'tion
nul'li fy	nul'li fy ing	nul'li fied	nul li fi ca'tion
qual'i fy	qual'i fy ing	qual' i fies	qual i fi ca'tion
grat'i fy	grat'i fy ing	grat'i fies	grat i fi ca'tion
clas'si fy	clas'si fy ing	clas'si fied	clas'si fi ca tion
ac com'pa ny	ac com'pa ny ing	ac com'pa nied	ac com'pa ni ment
cop'y	cop'y ing	cop'ied	cop'y ist
com ply'	com ply'ing	com plies'	com pli'ance
de fy'	de fy'ing	de fies'	de fi'ance
re ly'	re ly'ing	re lies'	re li'ance
hast'y	hast'i ly	hap'py	hap'pi ly
dain'ty	dain'ti ness	heart'y	heart'i ly
clean'ly	clean'li ness	sat'is fac to ry	sat is fac'to ri ly
beau'ty	beau'te ous	boun'ty	boun'te ous
mer'ry	mer'ri ly	haugh'ty	haugh'ti ly
pit'y	pit'e ous	du'ty	du'te ous

Word Building

Add the suffixes *ed* and *ing* and give the rule:

plan	assure	prevail	admit
hope	control	benefit	acquit
limit	conceal	commit	divert

LESSON 39

Plural of Nouns

Rule 5—Nouns regularly form their plurals by adding *s*, but *es* is added when the word is easier to pronounce than it would be with *s;* as, *book, books; bench, benches.*

Rule 6—Nouns ending in *y* preceded by a consonant form their plurals by changing *y* to *i* and adding *es;* as, *lady, ladies; company, companies.*

Rule 7—Nouns ending in *y* preceded by a vowel form their plurals by adding *s;* as, *valley, valleys; attorney, attorneys.*

(For additional rules, see rules 8, 9 and 10, page vi.)

Teacher: Pronounce forty words from the first and third columns and have the students write the plurals.

al ly'	al lies'	stu'di o	stu'di os
al'ley	al'leys	mot'to	mot'toes
tur'key	tur'keys	tor na'do	tor na'does
mon'key	mon'keys	so'lo	so'los
lil'y	lil'ies	pi an'o	pi an'os
the'o ry	the'o ries	car'go	car'goes
trag'e dy	trag'e dies	dy'na mo	dy'na mos
hol'i day	hol'i days	pro vi'so	pro vi'sos
pol'i cy	pol'i cies	ve'to	ve'toes
chim'ney	chim'neys	he'ro	he'roes
fac'ul ty	fac'ul ties	match	match'es
jour'ney	jour'neys	proof	proofs
fac'to ry	fac'to ries	brief	briefs
his'to ry	his'to ries	be lief'	be liefs'
pul'ley	pul'leys	loaf	loaves
cen'tu ry	cen'tu ries	leaf	leaves
at tor'ney	at tor'neys	knife	knives
po ta'to	po ta'toes	life	lives
to ma'to	to ma'toes	thief	thieves
fo'li o	fo'li os	shelf	shelves

Word Building

Add *ed, ing,* and *ence,* and tell why the final letter is or is not doubled:

refer	defer	prefer	excel
confer	concur	occur	infer

LESSON 40 (Oral)

Note—See Lesson 20 for the suffixes *ly* and *ity*, and Lesson 34 for *ize*.

ADJECTIVES	ADVERBS	VERBS	NOUNS
civ′il	civ′il ly	civ′i lize	ci vil′i ty
e′qual	e′qual ly	e′qual ize	e qual′i ty
le′gal	le′gal ly	le′gal ize	le gal′i ty
lo′cal	lo′cal ly	lo′cal ize	lo cal′i ty
mo′ral	mor′al ly	mor′al ize	mo ral′i ty
mor′tal	mor′tal ly	mor′tal ize	mor tal′i ty
re′al	re′al ly	re′al ize	re al i za′tion
mu′tu al	mu′tu al ly	mu′tu al ize	mu tu al′i ty
sol′emn	sol′emn ly	sol′em nize	so lem′ni ty
neu′tral	neu′tral ly	neu′tral ize	neu tral′i ty
spe′cial	spe′cial ly	spe′cial ize	spe′cial ty
lib′er al	lib′er al ly	lib′er al ize	lib er al′i ty
crit′i cal	crit′i cal ly	crit′i cize	crit′i cism
ma te′ri al	ma te′ri al ly	ma te′ri al ize	ma te ri al′i ty
dra mat′ic	dra mat′i cal ly	dram′a tize	dra′ma
the o ret′i cal	the o ret′i cal ly	the′o rize	the′o ry
per′son al	per′son al ly	per′son al ize	per son al′i ty
e co nom′i cal	e co nom′i cal ly	e con′o mize	e con′o my
fa mil′iar	fa mil′iar ly	fa mil′iar ize	fa mil i ar′i ty
na′tion al	na′tion al ly	na′tion al ize	na tion al′i ty
nec′es sa ry	nec′es sa ri ly	ne ces′si tate	ne ces′si ty
gen′er al	gen′er al ly	gen′er al ize	gen er al′i ty
sys tem at′ic	sys tem at′i cal ly	sys′tem a tize	sys′tem
pop′u lar	pop′u lar ly	pop′u lar ize	pop u lar′i ty
nat′u ral	nat′u ral ly	nat′u ral ize	nat u ral i za′tion

Civil, pertaining to the affairs of a city or government, courteous; *legal*, in conformity with law; *moral*, pertaining to right and wrong; *mortal*, subject to death, fatal; *mutual*, reciprocal, joint, common; *neutral*, not assisting either side, unbiased; *liberal*, generous, broad-minded; *critical*, exercising careful judgment, crucial; *material*, important, essential; *theoretical*, speculative, not practical; *economical*, frugal, thrifty; *national*, pertaining to a nation; *necessary*, not to be done without, indispensable; *general*, common to many, though not universal; *systematic*, acting according to a regular method or plan, methodical; *popular*, held in esteem by large number of people.

LESSON 41

Words Having *ie* and *ei*

Rule—"*I* before *e*, except after *c*, or when sounded like *a*, as in *neighbor* and *weigh*."

Teacher: Select forty words from the four columns and the exceptions.

be lieve'	niece	thief	de ceive'
re lieve'	re prieve'	shriek	de ceit'
yield	be lief'	field	per ceive'
grief	re lief'	piece	ceil'ing
brief	pierce	wield	weigh
chief	re view'	fierce	freight
a chieve'	fron'tier	con ceive'	neigh'bor
friend	mis'chief	con ceit'	sleigh
shield	be siege'	re ceive'	reign
re trieve'	fiend	re ceipt'	skein

Exceptions:

lei'sure	weird	for'eign	sur'feit
ei'ther	in vei'gle	sleight	for'feit
nei'ther	seize	sov'er eign	coun'ter feit

Achieve, to accomplish, to bring about a desired result; *retrieve*, to recover, to regain; *reprieve*, temporary delay in the execution of a sentence; *besiege*, to surround with armed orces, to press upon all sides; *conceive*, to comprehend, to understand; *perceive*, to obtain knowledge of through the senses, to discern; *skein*, a quantity of thread, silk, etc., coiled together; *weird*, strange and mysterious; *inveigle*, to persuade, especially to something evil, to entrap; *surfeit*, excess, especially in eating or drinking.

Words ending in *sede, ceed* and *cede*

1	supersede	3	exceed proceed succeed	7	accede cede concede intercede precede recede secede	

LESSON 42

Words Ending in *tion* and *sion*

Note—*Tion* and *sion* are noun suffixes, denoting *state, action, result of an act.*

Principle 1—Nouns derived from verbs ending in *te* usually take the ending *tion.*

Principle 2—Nouns derived from verbs ending in *ss, se, mit,* or *de* usually take the ending *sion.*

Teacher: Pronounce the words in the second and fourth columns.

em′u late	em u la′tion	o mit′	o mis′sion
fu′mi gate	fu mi ga′tion	ad mit′	ad mis′sion
ar′bi trate	ar bi tra′tion	per mit′	per mis′sion
stip′u late	stip u la′tion	sub mit′	sub mis′sion
a dul′ter ate	a dul ter a′tion	re mit′	re mis′sion
re pu′di ate	re pu di a′tion	cor rode′	cor ro′sion
im pute′	im pu ta′tion	de cide′	de ci′sion
com pute′	com pu ta′tion	de ride′	de ri′sion
re fute′	ref u ta′tion	col lide′	col li′sion
com press′	com pres′sion	se clude′	se clu′sion
dis cuss′	dis cus′sion	e lude′	e lu′sion
di gress′	di gres′sion	al lude′	al lu′sion
trans gress′	trans gres′sion	con cede′	con ces′sion
re press′	re pres′sion	ac cede′	ac ces′sion
pre cise′	pre ci′sion	per suade′	per sua′sion
in fuse′	in fu′sion	de lude′	de lu′sion
con fuse′	con fu′sion	ex clude′	ex clu′sion
pro fuse′	pro fu′sion	con clude′	con clu′sion
im merse′	im mer′sion	e vade′	e va′sion
a verse′	a ver′sion	in vade′	in va′sion

Emulate, to strive to equal or excel; *fumigate,* to disinfect by smoke or fumes; *arbitrate,* to submit to arbitrators for settlement; *stipulate,* to specify as the terms of an agreement; *adulterate,* to make impure by mixing in a baser substance; *repudiate,* to renounce, to disavow; *impute,* to attribute, as a fault or virtue; *refute,* to prove to be false or wrong; *digress,* to turn aside from the main subject of a discourse; *transgress,* to break a law, rule, etc.; *profuse,* very abundant or copious; *averse,* opposed to, unwilling; *corrode,* to eat away gradually by chemical action; *deride,* to ridicule; *allude,* to refer to indirectly.

LESSON 43

Words Ending in *tial, cial, tious, cious, gious*

Note—*Tial* and *cial*, pronounced *shăl; tious, cious, sious, xious*, pronounced *shŭs; gious* and *geous*, pronounced *jŭs*, are adjective terminations.

Principle 1—Adjectives derived from words ending in *t* or *nce* take the ending *tial;* as, *part, partial; prudence, prudential.* Adjectives derived from words ending in *ce*, except *nce*, take the ending *cial;* as *office, official.*

Principle 2—Adjectives having corresponding nouns ending in *tion* take the ending *tious;* as, *sedition, seditious.* Adjectives having corresponding nouns ending in *ce* or *city* take the ending *cious;* as, *vice, vicious; vivacity, vivacious.*

Teacher: Pronounce the words in the second and fourth columns.

po'tent	po ten'tial	am bi'tion	am bi'tious
pres'i dent	pres i den'tial	cau'tion	cau'tious
con'fi dent	con fi den'tial	vex a'tion	vex a'tious
dif'fer ent	dif fer en'tial	con ta'gion	con ta'gious
es'sence	es sen'tial	nau'se a	nau'seous
cre'dence	cre den'tials	re li'gion	re li'gious
of'fice	of fi'cial	te nac'i ty	te na'cious
jus'tice	ju di'cial	au dac'i ty	au da'cious
com'merce	com mer'cial	pre coc'i ty	pre co'cious
in'flu ence	in flu en'tial	vice	vi'cious
sub'stance	sub stan'tial	space	spa'cious
res'i dence	res i den'tial	ca price'	ca pri'cious
pref'er ence	pref er en'tial	av'a rice	av a ri'cious
prov'i dence	prov i den'tial	a troc'i ty	a tro'cious
cir'cum stance	cir cum stan'tial	fe roc'i ty	fe ro'cious
ar'ti fice	ar ti fi'cial	fal'la cy	fal la'cious
ben'e fit	*ben e fi'cial*	sus pi'cion	sus pi'cious
pal'ace	*pa la'tial*	su per sti'tion	su per sti'tious
fi nance'	*fi nan'cial*	in fec'tion	in fec'tious
prov'ince	*pro vin'cial*	fic'tion	fic ti'tious

Note—The words printed in italics are exceptions to the principles.

Credentials, that which certifies one's authority or claim to confidence; *artifice*, artful, skillful contrivance, trickery; *caprice*, a sudden unreasonable change, whim; *avarice*, excessive desire of gain; *tenacious*, holding fast, sticky, unyielding; *precocious*, prematurely developed; *fallacy*, false reasoning, error, delusion.

LESSON 44

Words Ending in *tient, cient, sient*

Tient, cient, sient, pronounced *shĕnt,* as adjective suffixes mean *being* or *doing;* as noun suffixes, they mean *one who* or *that which.*

pa′tient, forbearing; lenient; one under medical treatment.

ap pro ba′tion, approval; commendation; sanction.

im pos′tor, a pretender; deceiver.

suf fi′cient, equal to the need; adequate; enough.

bag′gage, luggage; the trunks, packages, etc., of a traveler.

pro fi′cient, thoroughly qualified.

an tiq′ui ty (-tĭk′wĭ-), state or quality of being ancient.

in cen′tive, motive; inducement.

e go tis′ti cal, manifesting self-exultation.

sal′u ta ry, healthful; wholesome.

of fi′ci ate (-shĭ āt-), to perform official duties.

shape′less, without definite shape.

nom′i nal, existing in name only; inconsiderable.

nine′ty, eighty-nine and one more.

quo′tient, the result obtained by dividing one number by another.

eu′lo gize (ū′-), to praise highly.

med′i cal, pertaining to the science or art of medicine.

spon ta′ne ous, acting through one's own impulse; voluntary.

im promp′tu, without preparation.

mer′it, to deserve something; worth; excellence.

de fi′cient, lacking some element of completeness; insufficient.

ar′bi tra ry, depending on the will or discretion; despotic.

u nique′, unparalleled; uncommon.

tran′sient, staying for a short time; brief; fleeting.

pes si mis′tic, inclined to look on the dark side of things.

an′cient, old-fashioned; antique.

sub stan′ti ate (-shĭ āt-), to establish the truth of; to verify.

mod′ern ize, to make modern.

wheth′er, which one of two; in case.

vis′i tor, one who makes a visit.

al ter′na tive (ăl-; âl-), a choice of two things or possibilities.

bar′ring, excluding by exception.

ad ver′si ty, affliction; calamity; misfortune.

ef fi′cient, productive of results.

ex ter′mi nate, to destroy utterly; to expel; to annihilate.

pos′i tive ly, definitely; expressly.

fric′tion, a rubbing together of two bodies; irritation.

sup ple men′ta ry, serving to supply what is lacking; additional.

wrap′per, an outward covering.

im pet′u ous, vehement in feeling; hasty; impulsive.

LESSON 45

Words Reviewing Principles

ic to'ri ous, having gained a victory; triumphant.

ab'er na cle, a house of worship; a tent.

e nounce'ment, act of renouncing.

am en ta'tion, audible expression of sorrow.

ru den'tial, marked by careful thought or wisdom.

ub mit'ting, yielding; resigning.

u'ti cle, the outer skin; the epidermis.

id'dance, the act of freeing.

i ver'sion, recreation; entertainment.

ex a'tious, causing irritation or annoyance.

m pa'tient, not patient; restless.

ol lab'o ra tor, one who works or acts jointly with others.

et'i cent, inclined to keep silent; uncommunicative.

x trav'a gant, wasteful; lavish.

a'di us, half the diameter of a circle.

e tach'a ble, capable of being separated or disconnected.

e mor'al ize, to corrupt in morals; to disorganize.

om mis'sion, to empower; authority to act; compensation.

ur'ried ly, in a hasty manner.

rev'a lence, state of being widespread or common.

in'cu bus, anything that oppresses or burdens.

nu mer'i cal, pertaining to numbers.

re nounc'ing, giving up; rejecting.

lam'en ta ble, expressing grief; pitiable; doleful.

su per fi'cial, pertaining to the surface; not deep; shallow.

ben'e fit ed, profited; helped.

physical, pertaining to nature; material; bodily.

con cealed', hidden; kept secret.

di vert'i ble, capable of being diverted.

sa ga'cious, keen; shrewd; having good judgment.

pro fi'cient, thoroughly qualified.

ex tin'guish er, one who or that which puts out or destroys.

neg'li gent, inclined to omit what ought to be done; heedless.

sig nif'i cant, full of meaning.

la bo'ri ous, requiring labor; industrious.

in tan'gi ble, incapable of being touched or grasped; vague.

guise (gīz), the external appearance; dress; behavior.

ab bre vi a'tion, a shortened form of a word or phrase.

sim'pli fy ing, making plain.

va'can cy, state or condition of being vacant or empty.

LESSON 46

Some Useful Suffixes

Adjective Suffixes: **an, ian, ar, ary, ory** = *pertaining to*

Noun Suffixes: { **an, ian, ar, ary, ory** = *one who* or *that which*
{ **ary, ery, ory** also = *the place where*

ly ce′um, a literary association.

sub ur′ban, pertaining to the outlying districts of a city.

lax′i ty, state of being loose.

cy′clone, a storm characterized by high rotating winds.

com punc′tion, regret; remorse.

Ca na′di an, pertaining to Canada; a native of Canada.

a′cre age, area in acres.

di rec′to ry, classified list of names and addresses.

ob′du rate, stubborn; obstinate.

sec′ond a ry, subordinate; second-rate.

des′ti tute, without means.

guard′i an, one who has the care of another.

jer′sey, a kind of knitted jacket.

li bra′ri an, one who has charge of a library.

at test′, to certify; to vouch for.

duc′tile, capable of being drawn out into threads.

hid′e ous, shocking; dreadful.

reg′is trar (trär), one who registers; a keeper of records.

ac qui si′tion, act of acquiring.

aug′ment, to increase; to enlarge.

top′ic, a subject of discourse.

A mer′i can, pertaining to America; a native of America.

laud′a to ry, expressing praise.

em broid′er y, needlework to ornament fabrics, etc.

mag′ni fy ing, act of enlarging.

pos′ture, attitude; position of parts of the body.

sec′u lar, worldly; not sacred.

el e men′ta ry, pertaining to first principles; introductory.

in ces′sant, without ceasing.

de fault′, to fail to perform or to pay.

at tract′, to draw toward; entice.

ad′ver sa ry, an antagonist; an opponent.

prom′i nent, eminent; important.

in′fa mous, having a very bad reputation.

am′pli fy, to make more intense.

bind′er y, a place where books are bound.

as ton′ish, to surprise greatly.

plac′ard, a notice posted in a public place.

apt′i tude, general fitness.

a cute′, mentally keen; intense.

LESSON 47

Noun Suffixes

eer, ier, ist = *one who* or *that which*
ee = *one to whom* or *one on whom*
acy, ism, ure = *state, act* or *quality of*

vol un teer′, one who offers his services voluntarily.

pro′rate, to divide proportionately.

fin an cier′, one skilled in financial affairs.

trip′li cate, threefold; triple.

cap′i tal ist, one who has large property.

ac′tu al, existing in fact; real.

pay ee′, one to whom money is, or is to be, paid.

ac′tu ate, to incite to action.

ad′e qua cy, sufficiency for a purpose.

in val′i date, to make null.

pes′si mism, a disposition to take a gloomy view of things.

ter′mi nal, the end; extremity.

auc tion eer′, one who sells at auction.

pleas′ure, amusement in general.

cash ier′, one who has charge of money.

ve loc′i ty, rate of motion; speed.

cli en tele′ (-tĕl′), followers.

op′ti mist, one who looks on the bright side of things.

ap pall′, to terrify; to shock.

ad he′sive, sticky; holding fast.

pat ent ee′, one to whom a patent is granted.

re trench′, to cut down expenses.

su prem′a cy, the state of being supreme.

ab rupt′, sudden; hasty; steep.

fa′vor it ism, a favoring unfairly; partiality.

de part′ure, act of going away.

ref er ee′, one to whom a thing is referred for settlement.

as sign′, to allot; to appoint.

ma chin′ist, one who makes or repairs machinery.

sun′dries, various things.

op′ti mism, a disposition to take a hopeful view of things.

al lure′, to attract; to entice.

her′o ism, qualities of being a hero or heroine.

ap pend′, to attach; to annex.

draw ee′, one on whom an order for money is drawn.

co part′ner, a partner.

ap plaud′, to approve; to praise.

ad mo ni′tion, an expression of advice or warning.

sun′dry, several; various.

del′i ca cy, a luxury; refinement.

LESSON 48

Some Useful Prefixes

dis = *not,* or *the opposite act*
mis = *wrong* or *wrongly*
non = *not*

un = *not, opposite act*
in (**ig, il, ir, im**) = *not, in, into*
pro = *for, forward, before*

dis ap point', to defeat of hope; to frustrate.

mis state', to state wrongly.

im'mi grant, one who comes into a country to live.

im mor'tal, not subject to death.

non com mit'tal, not revealing one's opinion or purpose.

dis in her'it, to deprive of an inheritance.

dis a gree', to fail to agree.

il log'i cal, contrary to sound reasoning.

in dis creet', imprudent; unwise.

non'sense, that which is without sense.

mis sent', sent incorrectly.

pro ject', to throw or cast forward.

pro voke', to call forth; to irritate.

un sta'ble, not stable; unsteady.

mis tak'en, misunderstood; erroneous.

ig no'ble, not noble; degraded.

in ac'cu rate, incorrect; inexact.

non en'ti ty, a person of little or no account.

ir re proach'a ble, blameless; incapable of being condemned.

ir rep'a ra ble, not capable of being repaired or restored.

ir re fut'a ble, indisputable; unanswerable.

dis ap pear', to pass from view.

non es sen'tial, not absolutely necessary.

im merse', to plunge into; to dip.

in for'mal, not according to custom; unceremonious.

in'grain, to dye before weaving; to fix deeply.

im mac'u late, spotless; pure.

un af fect'ed, without pretense; natural.

in ad'e quate, not sufficient.

mis place', to put in a wrong place.

un due', not due; unreasonable.

il lib'er al, not generous; narrow-minded.

im mov'a ble, incapable of being moved.

mis spell', to spell incorrectly.

in sol'vent, unable to pay one's debts.

non ar riv'al, failure to arrive.

un va'ry ing, without changing.

pro'noun, a word that stands for a noun.

im pa'tient, hasty; not possessed of or exercising patience.

im ma ture', not fully grown, developed or perfected.

LESSON 49

Some Useful Prefixes

re = *back, again*
fore = *before*
for = *from, away*

out = *beyond*
over = *above*
under = *beneath*

re call′, to call back; to recollect.

re ad just′, to adjust again.

re im burse′, to refund or pay back.

re coil′, to rebound; spring back.

re ca pit′u late, to restate briefly.

rec og ni′tion, act of recognizing.

rec′om pense, to repay; a compensation.

rec ol lect′, to call to mind.

rec′on cile, to cause to be friendly again; to adjust.

rec om mend′, to commend to favorable notice.

fore see′, to see or have knowledge of beforehand.

fore tell′, to tell beforehand.

fore go′, to deny one's self.

un fore seen′, not seen beforehand.

fore bode′, to foretell; portend.

fore cast′, to predict; to foresee.

fore close′, to shut out; to bar.

fore sight′, power of seeing in advance.

o′ver do, to do excessively; overtax; exaggerate; exhaust.

for bear′, to be patient; to refrain or abstain from.

fore′thought, a planning beforehand.

for sake′, to desert; to abandon.

out stand′ing, uncollected; unpaid.

o ver rate′, to rate too highly.

out′fit, a fitting out; equipment.

out′cast, one who is cast out; an exile.

out weigh′, to exceed in weight or value.

out′go ing, going out; leaving.

un′der writ er, one who underwrites insurance, etc.

o ver charge′, to charge an excessive price.

o ver draw′, to exaggerate; to draw in excess of one's credit.

un der charge′, to charge too little.

o ver head′, situated above; aloft

un der es′ti mate, to set too low a value on.

out′put, the quantity produced.

o ver bal′ance, to outweigh.

un der rate′, to rate too low.

o ver se′er, one who oversees; a superintendent.

o′ver due, delayed beyond proper time of arrival or payment.

fore′taste, a taste beforehand; anticipation.

LESSON 50
Some Useful Prefixes

bi = *two*
tri = *three*
mono = *one*
semi = *half*
per = *through*

sub = *under, beneath*
pre = *before*
post = *after*
ante = *before*
anti = *against*

sub or′di nate, lower in order, class, or rank.

pre paid′, paid in advance.

pref′ace, an introduction to a book, speech, etc.

bi′cy cle, a two-wheeled vehicle.

an ti cli′max, the opposite of climax.

pre ma ture′, happening before the proper time.

tri′an gle, a three-sided figure.

sub a′gent, an agent under a superior.

mon′o tone, not varied in tone.

bi month′ly, occurring once in two months.

pre sen′ti ment, a foreboding.

sem i an′nu al, half-yearly.

post date′, to date after the real time.

an te me rid′i an, before noon.

per vade′, to pass through.

an ti sep′tic, any substance that destroys disease germs.

mon′o rail, a single-rail track.

an tith′e sis, a contrast.

sem′i week ly, twice a week.

mo not′o nous, uttered in an unvarying tone; without change.

an te ced′ent, going before in time; preceding.

post-mor′tem, made after death.

an′te room, a room forming an entrance to another.

sub′ju gate, to subdue; conquer.

an′te date, to date before the true time.

sub di vi′sion, a part made by subdividing a thing.

post pone′, to put off; to defer.

per en′ni al, lasting through the year.

an te mor′tem, before death.

bi en′ni al, taking place once in two years.

pre lim′i na ry, introductory.

per′co late, to ooze through.

tri en′ni al, occurring every three years.

an′ti dote, a remedy for poison.

per ceive′, to discern; to see.

tri′cy cle, a three-wheeled velocipede.

sem′i cir cle, one-half of a circle.

an tip′a thy, a strong dislike.

tri′ple (trĭp″l), threefold.

post′script, a paragraph added to a letter after it is concluded.

LESSON 51
Some Useful Prefixes

inter = *between, among*
multi (mult) = *many*
intro = *within*
super = *above, more than*
retro = *backward*

ex (e) = *out of, off*
extra = *beyond, outside of*
contra (contro, counter) = *against*
trans = *across, through, over*
circum (circu) = *around*

trans port', to carry from one place to another.

ex'tri cate, to free from difficulties or entanglements.

e merge', to come out into view.

in ter na'tion al, between or among nations or their citizens.

ret'ro grade, to go backward.

in tro duc'tion, a presentation.

con'tra band, forbidden to be brought in; smuggled goods.

ex-pres'i dent, one who has been president.

ex traor'di na ry, remarkable.

ret ro spec'tion, act of looking back on past things.

con'tro ver sy, dispute or debate.

in ter ur'ban, between cities or towns.

su per fi'cial, shallow; hasty.

tran scend', to rise above.

cir' cum stances, conditions or facts of a matter or subject.

e lic'it, to draw out or forth.

coun ter act', to neutralize.

cir'cu late, to move around.

mul ti plic'i ty, a great number.

trans at lan'tic, beyond the Atlantic.

re tro ac'tive, altering the result of past action.

in ter change'a ble, capable of being interchanged.

trans pose', to change the order.

coun ter bal'ance, to oppose with an equal weight or power.

in ter cept', to stop; to check.

in tro spec'tion, self-examination.

em'i grate, to leave one's country to settle in another.

in ter line', to write or insert between lines.

mul'ti tude, a great number.

in'ter state, existing between or including different states.

in ter fere', to interpose.

su per a bun'dant, abounding to excess.

su per'flu ous, excessive; needless.

coun ter mand', to cancel; revoke.

cir cum'fer ence, the distance around a circular body.

il lic'it, unlawful; improper.

su per vise', to superintend.

in ter sect', to cross each other.

mul'ti ply, to increase in number.

trans lu'cent, allowing light to pass through.

LESSON 52

Words Likely to be Confused

ac cept', to receive; to agree to.
ex cept', to leave out; to omit.

a dapt', to make suitable.
a dopt', to take as one's own.
a dept', an expert; proficient.

ad di'tion, that which is added.
e di'tion, the number of copies printed.

ad vice', counsel; information.
ad vise', to counsel; give advice.

af fect', to act upon; influence.
ef fect', to accomplish; a result.

as sist'ants, those who assist.
as sist'ance, help; aid; support.

at tend'ance, act of attending.
at tend'ants, those who attend.

choose, to make a choice.
chose, did choose.

com'ple ment, that which completes.
com'pli ment, delicate flattery; to praise.

co-op er a'tion, joint action.
cor po ra'tion, a legal business body or organization.

core, heart; the center.
corps (kōr), section of any army.
corpse, a dead body.

cor re spond'ence, intercourse by letters.
cor re spond'ents, those who correspond.

cred'i ble, worthy of belief.
cred'it a ble, meritorious; estimable.

de vice', a contrivance; a design.
de vise', to invent; to plan.

e lic'it, to draw out or forth.
il lic'it, unlawful; improper.

el'i gi ble, qualified; suitable.
il leg'i ble, not easily read.

e lim'i nate, to exclude.
il lu'mi nate, to light up.

em'i nent, distinguished; conspicuous.
im'mi nent, threatening; impending.

there'for, for this or that.
there'fore, on that account; hence.

Supplementary

Observe that each of the following words is spelled with one *l*:

repel	**propel**	**compel**	**excel**
impel	**dispel**	**expel**	**rebel**

LESSON 53

Words Likely to be Confused

ex cep'tion a ble, open to objection.

ex cep'tion al, superior; extraordinary.

ex pect', to anticipate; to look for.
sus pect', to surmise; to mistrust.

loose, unbound; to release.
lose, to suffer loss; to mislay.

in cite', to stir up; to spur on.
in'sight, mental vision.

for'mal ly, according to custom.
for'mer ly, previously.

far'ther, more distant.
fur'ther, additional; more in detail.

in'stance, an example; suggestion.
in'stant, of the present month.

la'ter, at a subsequent time.
lat'ter, opposed to former.

par ti'tion, a dividing wall.
pe ti'tion, an earnest request.

prac'ti ca ble, capable of being done.
prac'ti cal, useful; not theoretical.

prec'e dent, an example; a model.
pres'i dent, one who presides.

prin'ci pal, chief; money at interest.
prin'ci ple, a fundamental truth.

proph'e cy, a prediction.
proph'e sy, to predict.

pro pose', to offer for consideration.
pur'pose, to intend; intention.

re spect'ful ly, in a respectful manner.
re spec'tive ly, relating to each.

sta'tion a ry, not moving.
sta'tion e ry, paper, pens, etc.

sta'ble, firmly established; durable.
sta'ple, regularly produced; chief.

stat'ue, a modeled likeness.
stat'ure, height of the body.
stat'ute, a legislative enactment.

car'at, a twenty-fourth part.
car'et, a mark used in writing.
car'rot, an edible vegetable.

Word Building

Add *es*, *ed* and *ing* to the following words:

verify	notify	modify	qualify
vary	specify	gratify	accompany
classify	pacify	ratify	amplify

LESSON 54

Words Likely to be Confused

ad her'ence, act of holding fast to.
ad her'ents, followers; supporters.

al lowed', permitted; approved.
a loud', audibly; loudly.

aught, anything.
naught, nothing; a cipher.
ought, to be under obligation.

av o ca'tion, occasional occupation.
vo ca'tion, regular occupation.

car'ton, a pasteboard box.
car toon', a pictorial drawing.

cloth, a woven fabric.
clothe, to dress; to cover.

dai'ry, place where milk is kept.
di'a ry, record of daily events.

de'cent, respectable; becoming.
de scent', act of descending.
dis sent', to differ in opinion.

di'vers, various; several.
di verse', different; unlike.

e lapse', to pass away, as time.
lapse, to become void.
re lapse', a falling back.

health'y, possessing health.
health'ful, conducive to health.

in gen'ious, talented; clever.
in gen'u ous, frank; candid.

last, final; at the end.
lat'est, last up to this time.

light'en ing, making less heavy.
light'ning, a flash of electricity.

loath, unwilling; reluctant.
loathe, to dislike greatly.

or'di nance, a law or regulation.
ord'nance, military equipment.

per'se cute, to oppress; to harass.
pros'e cute, to sue; to carry on.

pres'ence, state of being present.
pres'ents, gifts; things presented.

trea'tise, a literary composition.
trea'ties, agreements between nations.

Word Building

Form adverbs from the following adjectives:

real	vague	audible	primary
annual	lawful	definite	ordinary

Add the suffix *ful* to the following words:

duty	help	hope	neglect
care	mercy	health	beauty

LESSON 55

Homonyms

al'tar, a communion table.
al'ter, to change.

au'ger, a tool for boring.
au'gur, to foretell.

bail, surety; a handle.
bale, a bundle.

bare, uncovered; unadorned.
bear, an animal; to carry.

berth, a sleeping place.
birth, coming into life.

can'vas, a coarse cloth.
can'vass, to solicit.

cap'i tal, chief city; wealth.
cap'i tol, a state building.

ce're al, pertaining to grain.
se'ri al, pertaining to a series.

choir, a band of singers.
quire, 24 sheets of paper.

cite, to summon; to quote.
sight, sense of seeing.
site, position or situation.

coarse, not fine; unpolished.
course, route; career.

coun'cil, an assembly.
coun'sel, to advise; adviser.

cur'rant, a kind of fruit.
cur'rent, now passing; common.

cym'bal, musical instrument.
sym'bol, a type or emblem.

de sert', to abandon; to forsake.
des sert', last course at dinner.

du'al, twofold; double.
du'el, combat between two.

fair, just; beautiful.
fare, passage money; food.

fate, appointed lot.
fete, a festival or holiday.

feat, an unusual performance.
feet, the plural of foot.

cent, a coin.
sent, did send.
scent, to smell; an odor.

Word Building

Prefix *non, dis, mis, un, in, ig, il, ir,* or *im* to the following words:

sent	likely	liberal	adequate
civil	modest	legible	material
noble	appoint	elegant	rational
valid	solvent	affected	essential

LESSON 56

Homonyms

forth, forward; away.
fourth, next after the third.

gilt, covered with gold.
guilt, state of being guilty.

grate, frame to hold fuel.
great, large; important.

hoard, to store away.
horde, a vast multitude.

in dict', to charge with crime.
in dite', to compose; to write.

les'sen, to make less.
les'son, something to learn.

man'tel, shelf above a fireplace.
man'tle, a loose cloak.

mar'shal, an officer; to guide.
mar'tial, pertaining to war.

mean, contemptible; base.
mien, manner; air.

meat, flesh used as food.
meet, to come together.
mete, to measure.

met'al, a metallic mineral.
met'tle, quality of temperament.

med'al, a reward of merit.
med'dle, to interfere.

min'er, one who mines.
mi'nor, one under age; less.

passed, did pass.
past, time gone by.

peace, state of quiet; calm.
piece, a part of anything.

peal, to ring loudly.
peel, to remove the skin.

ped'al, a lever for the foot.
ped'dle, sell from door to door.

peer, to look closely; an equal.
pier, a landing place.

oar, implement for rowing.
ore, native mineral.
o'er, contraction of *over*.

pare, to peel thinly.
pair, a couple; to unite.
pear, a kind of fruit.

peak, the top of anything.
peek, to look slyly.
pique, to vex; vexation.

Word Building

Add *ist, er, eer, or, ant, ian,* or *ier* to the following words:

defend	motor	special	interview
advise	invest	auction	speculate
history	finance	success	extinguish

LESSON 57

Homonyms

rain, water from the clouds.
reign, to rule; royal authority.
rein, strap of a bridle.

raise, to lift up.
raze, to demolish; to destroy.

rap, a sharp, quick blow.
wrap, to inclose; a cloak.

right, correct; a privilege.
rite, a solemn ceremony.
wright, a workman.
write, to inscribe; to compose.

role, a part or character.
roll, to turn; to revolve.

shear, to cut or clip.
sheer, unmixed; utter.

sleight, skill; artful trick.
slight, frail; insignificant.

sole, part of the foot; only.
soul, spiritual nature of man.

stake, pointed stick; wager.
steak, a slice of meat.

steal, to take wrongfully.
steel, a kind of metal.

straight, not crooked.
strait, narrow; a pass.

suite, a series or set.
sweet, tasting like sugar.

tare, allowance; a weed.
tear, to pull apart; to rend.

their, belonging to them.
there, in that place.

to, in a direction toward.
too, more than enough; also.
two, one and one.

vain, conceited; useless.
vane, a weathercock.
vein, blood vessel; streak.

vice, an immoral habit.
vise, device for holding.

waist, part of the body.
waste, to use recklessly.

waive, to relinquish; to forego.
wave, to move to and fro.

ware, goods; merchandise.
wear, to have on.

Word Building

Add *able* or *ous* to the following words and tell why final *e* is retained or dropped:

service	change	courage	purchase
nerve	sale	manage	outrage
value	peace	desire	insure

LESSON 58

Note—The words in this lesson may be spelled in two ways. The preferable way, according to Webster's International Dictionary, is given in this lesson.

fi'ber, a slender filament.

in close', to surround; to put into an envelope.

mea'ger, scanty.

in clo'sure, that which is placed within something.

en twine', to wind around.

in dorse', to write on the back of; to sanction.

in quire', to ask about.

in trust', to give into faithful keeping.

re-en force', to strengthen.

en cum'brance, that which burdens; a lien on real property.

of fense', any cause of anger.

de fense', that which defends or protects.

pre tense', deception.

mor'tise, a hole made in wood through which a corresponding part fits.

in still', to impart gradually.

dis till', to obtain by heating, evaporating and condensing.

in stall', to put into position.

in stall'ment, the act of establishing; a portion of a debt payable at stated times.

en roll', to register.

ful fill', to carry into effect.

full'ness, state of being full.

lus'ter, brilliancy; splendor.

the'a ter, a building for dramatic performances.

cen'ter, the middle point.

me'ter, an instrument for measuring.

mi'ter, a slanting junction at the corners of mouldings, etc.

can'dor, openness; frankness.

hon'or, to regard with esteem or respect; integrity.

vig'or, physical or mental power.

en've lope (en'vĕ lōp), a cover or wrapper.

col'or, a pigment; to dye.

dis trib'u tor, one who or that which distributes.

drafts'man, one who makes mechanical plans, sketches, etc.

one self', the reflexive and emphatic form of the pronoun *one*.

sir'up, a thick liquid made of the juice of fruits boiled with sugar.

mold, to become spoiled by musty growth; the matrix in which anything is shaped.

trol'ley, a carriage running on an overhead rail.

crit'i cize, to judge as a critic.

dis patch', to send off; speedy performance.

ma nil'a, a hemp used for rope, paper, etc.

LESSON 59
Words Used in Business

busi'ness like, characterized by business qualities; thorough.

bul'wark (bool'wȧrk), any means of defense or protection.

be nev'o lent, charitable; kindly.

bar'ter, to trade by exchanging one commodity for another.

dis par'i ty, inequality; disproportion.

ac cord'ance, harmony; agreement.

brib'er y, the giving, offering, or accepting of a bribe.

ben e dic'tion, the act of blessing; a blessing.

be seech', to ask for earnestly.

ad vi'so ry (-zō-), having power to advise or suggest.

aus pi'cious, giving promise of success; propitious.

ad ven'ture, a bold undertaking.

excise', an inland duty or tax; to impose an excise on.

bur'den, thing borne with difficulty; to oppress.

ap par'ent, evident; obvious.

sten'cil, a perforated sheet for printing.

ap por'tion, to allot in just proportion.

slo'gan, a rallying cry.

ab sorb', to swallow up; to engross completely.

dor'mi to ry, a building having sleeping rooms.

bar ri cade', any barrier obstructing passage; to obstruct.

ben e fi'ci a ry (-fĭsh'ĭ ȧ rĭ), one who receives a benefit.

be nev'o lence, an act of kindness.

bro'ker age, the business, fee or commission of a broker.

dis turb'ance, confusion; act of disturbing.

com'pe tent, capable or qualified.

au di to'ri um, a large building for public meetings.

de pos'i to ry, a place where anything is deposited.

bur'nish, to make or become bright.

anx'ious (ănk'shŭs), deeply concerned; greatly troubled.

af flict', to cause pain or distress to body or mind.

mus'cu lar, strong; powerful.

buck'ram, a coarse fabric for stiffening garments.

ac quire', to obtain; to get as one's own.

fac'tor, a divisor; an agent.

pen i ten'ti a ry (-shȧ), a state prison.

an neal', to soften and render less brittle.

cus'to mer, a purchaser.

ap'a thy, lack of feeling; indifference.

ag'o ny, extreme pain of mind or body; anguish.

LESSON 60 (Oral)

Words ending in *er, or; able, ible*

See Lessons 32 and 33 for the suffixes *able* and *ible* and Lesson 35 for *or* and *er*.

ad vise'	ad vis'er	ad vise'ment	ad vis'a ble
al lege'	al leg'er	al le ga'tion	al lege'a ble
as sess'	as ses'sor	as sess'ment	as sess'a ble
col lect'	col lec'tor	col lec'tion	col lect'i ble
con firm'	con firm'er	con fir ma'tion	con firm'a ble
con vert'	con vert'er	con ver'sion	con vert'i ble
dis burse'	dis burs'er	dis burse'ment	dis burs'a ble
em'u late	em'u la tive	em u la'tion	em'u la ble
en dure'	en dur'er	en dur'ance	en dur'a ble
en joy'	en joy'er	en joy'ment	en joy'a ble
ex pand'	ex pand'er	ex pan'sion	ex pan'si ble
ig nite'	ig nit'er	ig ni'tion	ig nit'i ble
in sure'	in sur'er	in sur'ance	in sur'a ble
nav'i gate	nav'i ga tor	nav i ga'tion	nav'i ga ble
ob serve'	ob serv'er	ob ser va'tion	ob serv'a ble
pro duce'	pro duc'er	pro duc'tion	pro duc'i ble
sep'a rate	sep'a ra tor	sep' a ration	sep'a ra ble
trans form'	trans form'er	trans for ma'tion	trans form'a ble
dem'on strate	dem'on stra tor	dem on stra'tion	de mon'stra ble
trans late'	trans la'tor	trans la'tion	trans lat'a ble
trans mit'	trans mit'ter	trans mis'sion	trans mis'si ble
trans port'	trans port'er	trans por ta'tion	trans port'a ble
vi'o late	vi o la'tor	vi o la'tion	vi'o la ble
in cin'er ate	in cin'er a tor	in cin er a'tion	in cin'er a ble
in ves'ti gate	in ves'ti ga tor	in ves ti ga'tion	in ves'ti ga ble

Allege, to assert without proving; *convert,* to change or transform; *disburse,* to pay out, as money; *ignite,* to set on fire, to take fire; *transform,* to alter, to change; *demonstrate,* to make evident, to exhibit by way of proof; *translate,* to change from one language into another; *transmit,* to cause to pass over or through, transfer; *transport,* to carry from one place to another; *violate,* to break, as a law or an oath, to transgress; *incinerate,* to burn to ashes, to cremate; *investigate,* to find out by careful inquiry, to examine; *advisement,* consideration, deliberation; *confirmation,* the act of confirming or ratifying; *separation,* the act of parting, dividing, or withdrawing.

LESSON 61

Words Used in Business

as so ci a'tion, a society; a connection of ideas.

fore go'ing, occurring previously; preceding.

ex te'ri or, the outward surface.

ste nog'ra pher, one who writes shorthand.

pe cu'ni a ry (-nĭ ā rĭ), relating to money; monetary.

dy'na mite, a nitroglycerin explosive; to shatter with it.

em boss', adorn with raised work.

ac'cu rate, free from error; precise; exact.

con spir'a cy (-spĭr'), a plot or evil combination.

grad'u al ly, by degrees; slowly.

spas mod'ic, convulsive; acting fitfully.

lit'er a ture, the whole body of a nation's books or writings.

pro pri'e ty, fitness; correctness.

de lin'quent, neglectful of duty; due and unpaid.

par tic'i pate, to take part in; to share.

mis no'mer, a wrong name.

com mit'tee, an appointed body of persons.

an tag'o nize, to oppose actively.

phi lan'thro py, love or benevolence toward mankind.

ap prox'i mate, near to; resembling; nearly exact.

bed'rock, bottom or underlying rock; solid bottom.

lux u'ri ous, inclined to expensive indulgence.

pro pen'si ty, natural inclination.

re it'er ate, to repeat again and again.

ex on'er ate (ĕg zŏn'-), to free from blame or guilt.

co-or'di nate, to harmonize; equal; not subordinate.

rel'e vant, pertinent; fitting.

grate'ful, affording pleasure; thankful.

right'eous (rī'chŭs), virtuous; upright; just.

hu mil'i ate, to mortify; humble.

ben e fac'tor, one who confers benefits.

so ci'e ty, cultured people of a community; an association.

cus'tom a ry, common; habitual.

mil lion aire', a person worth a million or more.

in fer'i or, of lower rank; of poor quality.

at'om, a minute particle.

ac'cu ra cy, correctness; exactness; precision.

o'di ous, detestable; offensive.

Feb'ru a ry (-rōō-), the second month of the year.

Sa mar'i tan, one given to relieving the needy.

LESSON 62
Words Used in Business

cir cu′i tous,* going round in a circuit; roundabout.

cen′sor, an official examiner of publications.

pe′nal ize,* to put a penalty on.

ex pe′ri ence, knowledge gained by trial and practice.

sec re ta′ri al, pertaining to a secretary.

sub due′, to overpower; soften.

per func′to ry, acting mechanically; careless or indifferent.

al′ien ist, a specialist in mental diseases.

in ter vene′, to come between.

ac qui esce′ (ăk wĭ ĕs′), to consent or agree by silence.

om ni pres′ent, everywhere present at once.

om nip′o tent, all powerful.

pre pon′der ance, a superiority in influence, weight, etc.

pri′ma ri ly, in the first place; originally.

pe nu′ri ous, miserly; stingy.

dis cour′te ous (-cŭr-), offensively rude; uncivil.

ex ist′ence, continuance in life; actual occurrence.

hy poth′e sis, a supposition.

gran′ar y (grăn′-), a storehouse for grain.

sanc′tion, to confirm; approval.

im per′son a tor,* one who represents characters; an actor.

re ju′ve nate, to make young again; to invigorate.

nom′i nal ly, in name only.

ac cept′ance, approval; the act of taking what is offered.

sub stan′ti ate (-shĭ-), to prove; to verify.

for bear′ance, exercise of patience.

res er va′tion, act of reserving; that which is reserved.

pos ter′i ty, future generations; descendants.

in cred′u lous, refusing belief.

in cor′po rate, to embody; to form into a corporation.

re mov′al, the act of taking away; dismissal.

lu′mi nous, giving forth light.

an noy′ance, the act of causing vexation; that which annoys.

pa ral′y sis, loss of voluntary movement.

ex′e cute, to carry out; perform.

di lap′i dat ed, fallen into ruin through age or neglect.

e go tis′tic, inclined to praise or exalt oneself.

de fraud′, to cheat; to overreach.

ar′ti san (-zăn), a craftsman; a mechanic.

as cend′, to move upward; to rise.

* See Lessons 30, 34, and 35 for principles governing *ous*, *ize*, and *or*.

LESSON 63

Words Used in Business

an ni ver'sa ry, annual return of an important date.

pub lic'i ty, state of being open to common knowledge.

an ni'hi late, to destroy utterly.

sin'gu lar ly, in a singular manner; unusually.

ra'tion al (răsh'ŭn ăl), having reason or understanding.

so lic'it ous, anxious; apprehensive; concerned.

com mu'ni cate, to make known.

com mod'i ty, an article of merchandise.

gi gan'tic (jī găn'tĭk), immense; huge; tremendous.

vet'er an, one old in experience.

rep re sent'a tive, one who or that which represents.

sci en tif'ic, agreeing with the principles of science; exact.

pe rus'al (pĕ rōōz'ăl), the act of reading with care.

pre dom'i nate, to prevail; rule.

won't, a colloquial contraction of *will not*.

de spise (-spīz'), to hold in contempt; to scorn.

cru'el ty, inhuman treatment.

sac'ri fice, to give up for the sake of something; an offering.

de plor'a ble, sad, grievous.

re in state', to place again in possession; to reëstablish.

ves'ti bule, an inclosed entrance; an antechamber.

cum'ber some, unwieldy; cumbrous; burdensome.

te'di ous, tiresome; wearisome.

re new'al, act of beginning again or of making new.

cyn'ic al (sĭn'-), inclined to sneer at rectitude and virtue.

boun'ti ful, free in giving; liberal; plentiful.

com mem'o rate, to celebrate.

ab'ro gate, to annul or repeal by authority.

im plic'it (-plĭs-), unquestioning; unreserved.

su pe'ri or, of higher quality.

hon'or a ry, done as a sign of high esteem.

an'ec dote, a brief account of some incident; a short story.

au'di tor, one who examines and verifies accounts.

rec re a'tion, diversion; play.

en thu si as'tic (-zĭ-), ardently zealous.

dis sem'i nate, to spread broadcast; to dispense.

de co'rum, correct behavior.

sim plic'i ty, state or quality of being simple; silliness.

pat'ron age, support or favor.

func'tion, office; duty; ceremonious gathering or event.

LESSON 64

Words Used in Business

mis in ter'pret, to interpret erroneously.

bur'gla ry, the crime of housebreaking.

mag'i cal, seemingly supernatural.

cred'u lous, believing too readily; easily imposed upon.

nine'ti eth, next after the eighty-ninth.

mis con'strue (or -strue'), to misinterpret.

ob'vi ous, easily seen; evident.

mu'ci lage, a gummy fluid used to stick things together.

rhet'o ric, art of literary composition.

gra tu'i tous, without pay; free.

clem'en cy, mildness toward offenders.

pro'gram, list of exercises; plan of procedure.

gra tu'i ty, a present; a donation.

re gen'er ate, to give new life to; to reform completely.

un prec'e dent ed, unparalleled; unusual.

cos'tume, style of dress; dress.

mer'ce na ry, influenced by a desire for gain only.

stren'u ous, actively vigorous; energetic.

des ti na'tion, the end or goal.

con tig'u ous, touching or joining at the edge; adjacent.

ob'lig a to ry, binding in law or conscience.

re viv'al, renewal; a religious awakening.

ex em'pli fy, to show by example.

de te'ri o rate, to become impaired in quality; to degenerate.

caus'tic, sharp or severe; corrosive; sarcastic.

ex hil'a rate (ĕg zĭl'-), to make merry; to enliven.

fig'ur a tive ly, not literal.

jeal'ous, fearful of being supplanted in love or friendship.

a nal'o gous, resembling in certain respects.

en cir'cle, to surround; embrace.

dev'as tate, to lay waste; to desolate.

mis'sile, a weapon that is thrown; a projectile.

in nate', inborn; natural; native.

ex ten'u at ing, excusing or palliating; minimizing.

dis in'te grate, to break up or decompose.

prox im'i ty, immediate nearness.

on'er ous, burdensome; oppressive; troublesome.

re bel', to resist authority by force; to revolt.

com'rade, a close companion.

a sy'lum, an institution for the relief of the afflicted.

LESSON 65

Words Used in Business

con spic′u ous, in full view; prominent; striking.

au thor′i ta tive, supported by authority.

at ten′tion, the act of attending.

pi o neer′, one who goes before; an advance settler.

con ges′tion, overcrowded condition.

stat is ti′cian, one versed in statistics.

cal′um ny, false accusation maliciously made; slander.

gen′u ine, real; not counterfeit.

jun′ior (jōon′yẽr), younger; lower in standing or rank.

a nal′y sis, the separation of anything into its component parts.

con′scious, mentally awake; aware.

spu′ri ous, not genuine; false.

gov′er nor, one who governs.

sen′ior (-yẽr), elder; superior in dignity, rank or office.

co er′cion, act of compelling.

nev er the less′, notwithstanding; however.

pe tro′le um, a crude mineral oil from which kerosene, gasoline, etc., are derived.

fi del′i ty, faithfulness; loyalty.

fo′cus, to bring to a center; a central point.

com plex′ion, color and appearance of the skin, general aspect.

dis coun′te nance, to refuse to approve or countenance.

a non′y mous, of unknown name or authorship.

aus tere′, stern; severely simple.

sed′en ta ry, requiring much sitting; inactive.

con sen′sus, a general agreement; accord.

com mo′di ous, roomy; convenient; spacious.

pre-em′i nent, superior to others; highest in rank or quality.

as′pect, appearance; outlook; view.

psy chol′o gy (sī kŏl′ŏ jĭ), the science of the mind.

al′ter nate (ăl′-; ôl′-), a substitute; to take place by turns.

com pul′sion, subjection to force.

pon′der ous, very heavy; massive.

ap prais′er, one who evaluates.

ser′geant (sär′jĕnt), a noncommissioned officer.

ce les′tial, heavenly; divine.

al ter ca′tion (ăl-; ôl-), an angry dispute.

bi tu′mi nous, a term applied to any coal or other mineral containing bitumin.

cho′rus, a body of singers.

com pet′i tive, pertaining to competition or rivalry.

con sci en′tious, governed by conscience; scrupulous.

LESSON 66

Words Used in Business

ses'sion, a meeting of an organized body.

mer i to'ri ous,* praiseworthy; deserving of reward.

def'i nite ly, precisely; clearly.

ex'em pla ry (ĕg'zĕm-), serving as a model; commendable.

scan'dal, defamation; disgrace; a dissemination of evil reports.

ex punge', to blot or rule out; erase.

ob nox'ious (-nŏk'shŭs), offensive; unpopular.

sym pa thet'ic, having a fellow-feeling for others; congenial.

an i mos'i ty, hatred; ill will.

in ca pac'i tate, to make incapable; to disqualify.

ac count'an cy, the art of keeping or adjusting accounts.

stu'di ous, given to study.

in au'gu rate, to induct into office; to initiate.

a but'ment, the supporting structure at the end of a bridge.

per plex'i ty, condition of doubt.

dis par'age, to belittle; to speak of slightingly.

brand'-new, perfectly new.

ac count'ant, one skilled in keeping or adjusting accounts.

ex tort', to obtain by force.

vo ca'tion al, pertaining to a calling; an applied trade school.

ci'pher, a symbol denoting naught; to figure.

im mu'ni ty, freedom from any duty, tax, service, etc.

mon'o cle,* eyeglass for one eye.

ret ri bu'tion, suitable punishment for a wrong.

math e mat'i cal, pertaining to mathematics; rigidly exact.

o'dor, any smell; scent; a perfume.

pro pi'tious, kindly disposed; favorable; auspicious.

req'ui site (rĕk'wĭ zĭt), that which is required; indispensable.

vig'or ous, full of vigor; robust.

plu ral'i ty, excess of votes over the next highest.

va'gran cy, state of wandering without a settled home.

lu'di crous, comical; absurd.

im i ta'tion, the act of imitating; counterfeit.

com pul'so ry, required by authority; obligatory.

der'e lict, unfaithful; neglectful.

e qui lib'ri um, even poise or balance.

con'science, (-shĕns), sense of right.

pre ca'ri ous, subject to risk or danger; uncertain.

cru'cial, decisive; searching.

pro pri'e tor, one who has a legal right to anything; owner.

* See Lessons 30 and 31 for principles governing *ous* and *cle*.

LESSON 67
Words Used in Business

req ui si'tion, a formal demand or application.

in es'ti ma ble,* priceless; beyond measure or price.

rig'or ous, strict; severe; harsh.

con sid er a'tion, careful thought; deliberation.

chron'i cle, to record historical details; a register of events.

re vert', to return; to turn back.

ed'i tor, one who edits or has charge of a publication.

chem'i cal (kĕm'-), pertaining to chemistry.

im por'tant, of much consequence.

in dul'gent, yielding to the humor, wishes, etc., of another.

mu'si cal, pertaining to music; melodious; harmonious.

ve rac'i ty, truthfulness; truth.

dis sen'sion, discord; disagreement in opinion.

jus'ti fi a ble, capable of being justified; warrantable.

pre pos'ter ous, absurd; foolish.

im pen'e tra ble, not to be entered or penetrated.

cog'ni zance (-zănce), heed; notice; knowledge.

re tain, to keep; to employ.

om nis'cient (-nĭsh'ĕnt), knowing all things; infinitely wise.

lus'cious, delightful to the taste.

sig nif'i cance, meaning or import; consequence.

pro fes'sor, an instructor in a college or university.

pli'a ble, easily bent; flexible.

con sid'er a ble, rather large in amount, extent, etc.

co in'ci dent, exactly agreeing; happening at the same time.

change'a ble, variable; inconstant.

im per'ti nent, not to the point; insolent; disrespectful.

sac'ri lege (-lĕj), the profaning of anything sacred.

ar'ro gant, overbearing; haughty.

ten'sion, the state of being stretched; mental strain.

ir rev'o ca ble, incapable of being revoked; unalterable.

jan'i tor, caretaker of a building.

op'ti cal, pertaining to optics or vision.

con ten'tion, act of contending; strife; point in controversy.

ap'pli ca ble, suitable; appropriate.

ir rep'a ra ble, not capable of being repaired or restored.

in cal'cu la ble, beyond estimate; very great.

re ten'tion, act of retaining.

per vert', to turn from its right purpose, use, or meaning.

fu'ri ous, very angry; tempestuous.

* See Lesson 32 for principles governing *able.*

LESSON 68
Words Used in Business

de lib′er ate ly, done after full consideration; slowly.

u nan′i mous,* having the consent of all; of one mind.

phy si′cian (fĭ zĭsh′ăn), a doctor of medicine.

de mean′or, behavior; deportment.

com′a tose, a state of stupor; lethargy.

tyr′an ny (tĭr′ă nĭ), arbitrary or despotic exercise of power.

fab′u lous, fictitious; astonishing.

clas′sic, pertaining to the highest class in literature and art.

in tu i′tion, insight; instinctive knowledge.

suc cinct′, concise; terse; brief.

in vet′er ate, confirmed; deep-rooted.

junc′tion, a place of union or meeting.

o bit′u ar y, a death notice.

pro ba′tion, a period or state of trial.

in trin′sic, inherent; genuine.

pro cras′ti nate, to put off.

del′i cate, physically frail; refined.

ec cen′tric (ĕk-), erratic; whimsical; peculiar.

like′li hood, probability; a sign; an indication.

mo men′tum, force of a moving body.

res ur rec′tion, act of rising from the dead; renewal.

vi cis′si tude, change, as of circumstances or fortune.

char′la tan (shär′lă tăn), an impostor; a quack.

dex ter′i ty, skill; expertness.

pro lif′ic, fertile; producing abundantly.

a mal′ga mate, to mix or unite so as to form a uniform whole.

sanc′ti ty, sacredness; godliness.

pas′teur ize* (păs′tẽr īz), to free from germs by heating, as milk.

in′tri cate, involved; complicated; entangled.

de cep′tion, an artifice or fraud.

with hold′, to hold back; to refuse to grant.

an′ti quat ed, grown old; out of date.

co′pi ous, plentiful; abundant.

cau′ter ize, to burn or sear with caustic.

fas′ci nate, to charm; to captivate.

ap pren′tice, a learner; beginner.

sar cas′tic, cutting; sneering.

pul′ver ize, to reduce to a fine powder.

a bove′board, without concealment; openly.

com pen′di um, a summary; abstract.

* See Lessons 30 and 34 for principles governing *ous* and *ize*.

LESSON 69

Words Used in Business

pre′mi er, first in position or importance.

pre rog′a tive, exclusive privilege or right.

sym met′ri cal, in harmonious proportion.

con clu′sive, decisive; convincing.

rus′ti cate, to live temporarily in the country.

gaz et teer′, a dictionary of geographical names.

vo li′tion, act of willing; choice.

de rog′a to ry, tending to detract from or to disparage.

pol y tech′nic, pertaining to several arts or sciences.

in′ter val, space of time between.

sher′iff, the chief peace officer of a county.

prob lem at′ic al, questionable; uncertain.

fe lic′i ty, supreme happiness.

scin til′la (sĭn tĭl′à), a mere spark or glimmer.

prom′is so ry, containing a promise to do or not to do something.

re scind′, to cancel; to annul.

con grat′u late, to felicitate; to wish joy to.

ma tu′ri ty, state of being fully developed.

e lu′ci date, to make clear.

poign′ant (poin′-), sharp and piercing; bitter.

man u fac′ture, to make from raw materials.

ab sorp′tion, act of absorbing or soaking up.

in ten′sive, tending to give force or emphasis.

ob′sti nate, stubborn; headstrong.

whole′sale, buying or selling in quantity.

sal u ta′tion, a courteous greeting; the act of saluting.

in no va′tion, a change or novelty.

con gre ga′tion, an assembly for religious worship.

com men′su rate (-shoō), adequate; corresponding amount.

coun′ter claim, an opposing claim.

in ge nu′i ty, skill in devising or designing.

typ′ist, one who operates a typewriter.

le git′i mate, lawful; genuine.

in tim′i date, to frighten, especially by threats.

im prac′ti ca ble, incapable of being used or availed of.

ob lit′er ate, to destroy utterly.

rem′e dy, that which corrects, relieves, or cures.

il lit′er ate, unable to read or write; unrefined.

pre mo ni′tion, previous warning.

con ti nu′i ty, state or quality of being continuous.

LESSON 70
Words Used in Business

aq'ue duct, a conduit for conveying water.

ab hor'rence, a feeling or strong hatred; loathing.

con'sum mate (-sŭ-), to complete.

cam'bric (kām'-), a fine, thin, white linen fabric.

al loy', a mixture of a baser metal with a finer one.

cu'li na ry, pertaining to cooking.

ad o les'cent, approaching maturity; pertaining to youth.

ap peal', a call for aid or sympathy; entreaty.

crev'ice, a narrow opening; a crack.

con gen'ial (-jēn'yăl), agreeable; sympathetic.

ab sorb'ent, anything that absorbs; having the power to absorb.

co'gent, forcible; convincing.

a cu'men (a cū'-), keenness of insight or discernment.

a mends', compensation for injury; recompense.

cu'ri ous, inquisitive; mysterious.

a bu'sive, using harsh words; insulting.

bar'gain (-gĕn; -gĭn), an agreement; an advantageous purchase; to trade.

aus pi'cious, favorable; prosperous.

cor'ru gat ed, shaped into folds or ridges.

cour'te sy, politeness; civility.

a bom'i na ble, loathsome; detestable; odious.

con do'lence, an expression of sympathetic sorrow or grief.

con'tour (-tōōr), outline; profile.

am bas'sa dor, a diplomatic envoy of the highest rank.

ath let'ics, athletic games and exercises collectively.

am'i ca ble, friendly; peaceable.

ac quaint'ance, knowledge; a person with whom one is acquainted.

cre a'tive, having the power to create; productive.

dig'ni ty, stateliness of manner.

chas tise' (chăs tīz'), to correct by punishment.

con sec'u tive, following in regular order; successive.

de spond'ent, disheartened.

ad here', to stick fast; to become firmly attached.

ad vis'ed ly, deliberately; not hastily.

cor re spond', to agree; to match.

as say', to subject to assay or analysis.

bul'le tin (bōōl'ĕ tĭn), a brief statement of news to the public; a periodical.

con tra dic'to ry, inconsistent.

ap'pli cant, one who applies; a candidate.

as suage', to allay; to lessen.

LESSON 71

Words Used in Business

mu si'cian, one skilled in the art or science of music.

a bey'ance, holding back for a time; temporary inactivity.

lav'a to ry, a place to wash the hands, face, etc.

car'bon, a nonmetallic substance.

phi los'o phy, practical wisdom; branch of advanced learning.

sem'i na ry, a higher school, academy or college.

il lus'tri ous, distinguished.

o ver whelm', to overpower or crush completely.

vac'il late (văs'-), to fluctuate in mind; to waver.

cel'lar, an underground room.

ma tric'u late, to enroll as a member.

con nois seur' (kŏn ĭ sûr'; -sūr'), a competent judge of art, etc.

cem'e ter y, a burial place.

com pos'ite, made up of distinct parts; compounded.

vo cab'u la ry, the whole number of words used by an individual.

bou'le vard (bōō'lĕ), a broad avenue usually bordered with trees.

tu i'tion, charge for instruction.

quad'ru ple, to multiply by four; fourfold.

cu'mu la tive, increasing through addition.

fick'le, changeable; inconstant.

in co her'ent, inconsistent; without connection.

con vey'ance, means of transporting; a vehicle.

san i ta'ri um, a health resort; a sanatorium.

cur ric'u lum, a course of study.

ad dict'ed, strongly inclined to some object, practice, etc.

nick'el, a whitish metal; a five-cent coin.

live'li hood, means of living.

may'or, the chief official of a town or city.

in fin i tes'i mal (-tĕs'-), immeasurably small.

irk'some, tedious; wearisome.

o bey', to comply with orders or instructions.

gym na'si um (-nā'zĭ ŭm), a building for athletic exercises.

for lorn', deserted; destitute.

de gen'er ate, to decline in quality; to deteriorate.

dis cre'tion a ry, left to one's judgment or discretion.

in'sti ga tor, one who urges or incites to wrong-doing.

a void'ance, the act of evading.

com po'nent, a constituent part or ingredient.

dex'ter ous, skillful; done with dexterity.

e volve', to develop or unfold.

LESSON 72

Words Used in Business

as′sets, property in general, usable for paying debts.

dis so lu′tion, act of dissolving or breaking up.

co part′ner ship, a partnership.

ton′nage (tŭn′ȧj), amount of shipping estimated in tons.

book′keep er, one who keeps accounts.

san′i ta ry, pertaining to health.

in tel′li gent, possessed of a high degree of understanding.

ac cel′er ate, to quicken; hasten.

spon′sor, one who binds himself to answer for another.

bank′rupt cy, state of being unable to pay one's just debts.

ven′due, a public sale by auction.

prox′y, a document authorizing one person to act for another.

dic′tion a ry, a book containing the words of a language, their meanings and pronunciation.

a byss′, any space of vast depth.

dis fran′chise, to deprive of a legal privilege, as of voting.

tran′quil, quiet; calm; serene.

ci vil′i an (-yăn), one who pursues civil life.

sub sid′i a ry, furnishing aid.

em bar′go, a government edict prohibiting transportation.

col lat′er al, that which is pledged as security.

de mur′rage, a charge for delay in loading or unloading a car.

in debt′ed ness, state of being in debt.

def′al ca tor (-ăl-), an embezzler.

bro′ker, one who deals in money, stocks, bonds, etc.

ex ec′u tive, skilled in execution; an administrative officer.

de lin′e ate, to sketch; portray.

in′ven to ry, list of goods with their estimated worth.

dis crep′an cy, a disagreement.

due′bill, written acknowledgment of a debt.

con sign′or (-sīn′ẽr; sĭ nôr′), one who consigns something.

her met′i cal ly, closed; air tight.

pro mul′gate, to make known formally and officially; to publish.

ne go′ti ate (-shĭ-), to sell, as commercial paper or securities; to confer with others.

ro′ta ry, turning; revolving.

re ceiv′er, one who holds in trust property under litigation.

dis cord′ant, not in harmony.

div′i dends, a sum of money divided among shareholders.

ex or′bi tant, grossly excessive.

neg′li gi ble, of little account or value; unimportant.

con sign ee′ (-sī nē′), one to whom something is consigned.

LESSON 73

Words Used in Business

di men'sion, extent, as length, breadth, or thickness.

e val'u ate, to fix the value of; to appraise.

der'rick, an apparatus for lifting heavy weights.

ex ist'ence, state of existing.

ex clu'sive, excluding or tending to exclude.

ex pe'di ent, suitable; advisable; suitable means for an end.

in sur'gent, one who rebels against authority.

fran'chise, a particular privilege.

griev'ance, a cause of complaint; an injury.

guar'an tee (găr'-), to be responsible for; to warrant.

in ter rupt', to break the continuity or uniformity of.

de tour' (-to͞or'), a roundabout way.

ur'gent, calling for immediate attention; pressing.

ex pe'ri ence, knowledge gained by trial; something lived through.

gen'er ous, liberal; munificent.

per'emp to ry, admitting no refusal; decisive.

ab'scess, a collection of pus in the tissues of the body.

ex pend'i ture, disbursement; expense.

grat'i tude, state of being grateful; thankfulness.

dor'mant, temporarily inactive.

plaus'i ble, seeming to be true; specious.

per se ver'ance, act or state of not giving up; constant effort.

fas tid'i ous, hard to please; overnice.

frag'ile, easily broken; brittle.

i den'ti fy, to establish the identity of.

re sil'i ent (-zĭl'-), having the capacity to rebound; elastic.

pro spec'tus, an outline of a proposed undertaking.

gra'tis (grā'tĭs), without charge.

de li'cious, highly pleasing to the taste; delightful.

ad min'is ter, to manage or conduct, as public affairs; to dispense.

dom'i nant, ruling; controlling.

per'ma nent, continuing without change; stable.

Word Building

Write nouns ending in *tion* or *sion* from the following verbs:

acquire	require	provoke	reduce
convert	contend	preclude	suspend

LESSON 74

Words Used in Business

stor'age, safe keeping of goods; price for storing.

dep're cate, to express disapproval of.

ce ler'i ty, quickness; speed.

gab er dine' (-den'), a waterproof coat or cloth for making one.

bor'ough (bŭr'ō), an incorporated town or village.

tran scribe', to make a copy of.

o va'tion, a noisy demonstration of public esteem.

du plic'i ty, insincere conduct.

co lo'ni al, pertaining to a colony or colonies.

pes'ti lence, any virulent, widespread contagious or infectious epidemic disease.

co a li'tion, an alliance of persons, parties, or states.

met'a phor, a figure of speech.

buf fet' (bŏŏ fā'), a sideboard; a counter for refreshments.

gor'geous, showy; magnificent.

chif fo nier' (shĭf ŏ nēr'), a piece of furniture with drawers

prom'i nent, eminent; conspicuous

per se vere', to persist in any undertaking.

an nex', to unite or to connect.

con ven'tion al, formal; following set rules.

lit'er a ry, pertaining to literature or letters.

et'i quette (-kĕt), the usages of polite society.

con va les'cent, recovering health or strength.

ster'i lize, to free from germs.

di ag'o nal, having an oblique direction or extension.

lac'er ate (lăs'-), to tear raggedly; to wound.

mi'cro scope, a magnifying glass.

pas'tor, a clergyman having charge of a church.

de nom i na'tion, a sect or class.

cap'tain, the commander of a company.

ad min'is tra tor, one who settles the estate of a person dying without making a will.

prox'i mo, in or of the coming month.

du'pli ca tor, a copying machine.

half'-tone, a photographic process of making printing plates.

dis com mode', to inconvenience.

par quet' (-kā'), the lower floor of a theater.

pen'i tent, feeling sorry for sins.

in nu'mer a ble, too many to be counted.

mer'ci ful, full of mercy; mild.

pro spec'tive, relating to the future; expected.

can'di da cy, state of being a candidate.

LESSON 75

Words Used in Business

di rec'tor, one appointed to transact the affairs of a company.

con'gress, the national legislature of the United States.

un par'al leled, without an equal.

am mo'ni a, a pungent gas, readily soluble in water.

im'be cile, a weak-minded person.

cal'en dar, a register of the days, weeks, months of the year; a list of criminal cases for trial.

ma neu'ver, to manage with art and skill; to manipulate.

ex tol' (-tŏl'), to praise highly.

ros'trum, a platform for public speaking.

a dult', one of full age, size, etc.

fra ter'nal, pertaining to or befitting a brother.

sal'a ble, capable of being sold.

cel'lu loid, a compound of camphor and guncotton.

lathe, a machine for shaping wood or metal.

ed'u ca tor, a teacher or tutor.

Lloyd's, London corporation for carrying marine insurance, etc.

be hav'ior (-yĕr), deportment.

Chau tau'qua (shȧ tô'kwä), a system of education by summer schools and lectures.

a ro'ma, agreeable spicy odor.

bur'lap, a fabric of jute or hemp, used for bagging.

tur'bu lent, disorderly; uncontrollable; riotous.

hy drau'lic, pertaining to the science of liquids in motion.

be nig'nant, kind; genial; bland.

i'o dine, a drug used in medicine or in making dyes.

bane'ful, poisonous; pernicious.

mac ad'am ize, to build or finish a road by a compact layer of crushed stone.

rem i nis'cent, recalling or thinking much about the past.

be queath', to give by will.

lin'e al, pertaining to a line or lines.

cor'pu lent, bulky; extremely fat.

trac'tor, an engine for drawing farm machinery, etc.

op'u lent, very wealthy; rich.

junc'ture, the point where two bodies are joined.

mo'bi lize, to assemble for service, as troops.

do'nor, one who gives; a giver.

pic tur esque' (-ĕsk'), having wild, rugged, irregular beauty.

pen'u ry, extreme poverty; want.

lin'o type, a typesetting machine that casts each line of type in one piece.

kiln-dry, to dry in a kiln.

en tail', to impose as a necessary result.

LESSON 76
Words Used in Business

al le′giance (-jăns), fidelity to a cause or person; devotion.

pred e ces′sor, one who has preceded another in time.

pa′tience, forbearance; quality of being patient.

re pug′nant, repulsive; offensive.

oc′u list, one skilled in the treatment of eye diseases.

a cous′tic (-kōōs′-), pertaining to the science of sound; auditory.

ob serv′ance, the act of observing laws or customs.

ab′so lute ly, wholly; positively.

ba tiste′ (bȧ tēst′), a kind of fine cotton muslin.

ex ploit′, to use for one's own profit; heroic act.

de scend′ant, one who descends; an offspring.

e clipse′, to darken or conceal; to surpass.

ma lig′nant, disposed to do harm; virulent.

ju di′cious, wise; directed by sound judgment.

lac′quer (lăk′ēr), kind of varnish.

per cent′age, rate by the hundred; a part or portion of the whole.

hab er dash′er, a dealer in men's furnishings.

sus pend′, to cease for a time; to attach to something above.

kitch en ette′, a small room, combining kitchen and pantry.

jo′vi al, joyous; jolly; merry.

lab′o ra to ry, a place for making scientific experiments.

pro di′gious (-dĭj′ŭs), unusually great in size, extent, etc.

mag′ni tude, greatness, as in size, importance, etc.

de ten′tion, the act of detaining.

ex tor′tion, the act of obtaining by force or threat.

con demn′, to pronounce to be unfit for use; censure; doom.

in ci′sion, a cut made with a sharp instrument.

des′ig nate, to name; to point out.

nu′mer ous, consisting of a great many.

ef′fi ca cy, power to produce results; efficiency.

so lic′i tor, one who solicits.

meg′a phone, a device to magnify sound, as a large funnel.

Word Building

Write nouns in *cy* or *acy* from the following words:

supreme	**stringent**	**accurate**	**deficient**
delinquent	**competent**	**constituent**	**adequate**

LESSON 77

Words Used in Business

fo'rum, a gathering for public discussion.

debt'or, one who is under obligation to another.

re cruit', one who has just joined a cause; to obtain fresh supplies.

is'su ance, act of issuing.

pro'file, an outline, as of a face seen from the side.

reg'is ter, a book containing regular entries; to record.

prog'ress, a moving or going forward; development.

pre ten'sion, the act of pretending.

re sist'ance, the act or capacity of opposing; a striving against.

proc'ess, the act of going on; progress; advance.

rou tine' (rōō tēn'), a course of action regularly pursued.

de pos'i tor, one who deposits.

ex ten'sion, act of extending; enlargement.

en sem'ble (än sän'bl'), the whole; all the parts taken together.

per'jure, to violate one's oath.

graph'ic (grăf'-), lifelike; vividly described.

im pan'el, to enter on a panel; to enroll.

rec'og nize, to acknowledge formally; to know again.

re ha bil'i tate, to restore to a former state or rank; reinstate.

des'per ate, reckless; frantic.

prej u di'cial, detrimental; injurious; damaging.

ma jor'i ty, more than half of any total; of full legal age.

ex trav'a gance, excess, especially in spending money.

im par'tial, unbiased; fair; just.

man slaugh'ter, the killing of a human being without malice.

prov o ca'tion, act of provoking to anger; annoyance.

pre'cious (prĕsh'us), of great price or value; costly.

his tor'i cal, relating to history.

e quiv'a lent, equal in worth, value, power, etc.

de but' (dā bü'), the first appearance in society or in public.

su per vi'sor, overseer; inspector.

in cum'bent, required as a duty; one holding an office.

Word Building

Write the plural of the following nouns:

attorney	inquiry	valley	alley
quantity	journey	security	agency

LESSON 78

Words Used in Business

im pru'dent, lacking caution or discretion; indiscreet.

in'fan tile (-tĭl; -tīl), pertaining to an infant or infancy.

in dig'nant, angry because of unfair treatment.

in cep'tion, beginning; first stage.

col le'gi ate, pertaining to a college.

cen ten'ni al, pertaining to a hundred years, or to a hundredth anniversary.

in terne', a resident hospital physician or surgeon.

en com'pass, to surround; encircle.

clam'or, noisy confusion of voices; to cry out.

in i'tial, standing at the beginning; first; to mark with an initial.

cer tif'i cate, a written testimony to the truth of any fact.

eq'ui ty, justice; impartiality.

mo'men ta ry, continuing only a moment; transitory.

ques tion naire' (-âr'), a set of questions submitted to a number of persons in investigations, etc.

hu mid'i ty, moisture; dampness.

comp trol'ler (kŏn-), one who examines and certifies accounts.

im por'tance, quality or state of being important; significance.

cow'ard ice (-ĕr dĭs), unworthy timidity; lack of courage.

con'tem plate, to look forward to; to intend.

e pit'o me, a summary; a synopsis.

cham'ois (shăm'ĭ), a soft leather.

chap'er on (shăp'ĕr ōn), a woman who accompanies a young unmarried woman in public.

ker'o sene, a mineral oil produced from petroleum.

eq'ui ta ble, impartial; just.

die, a device for shaping or imprinting.

in i'ti ate (-ĭsh'ĭ āt), to originate; to introduce into a club, etc.

bro chure' (brŏ shür'), a brief treatise in pamphlet form.

en tice', to attract or allure.

sew'er (sū'ĕr), an underground pipe for carrying off sewage.

cam'er a, an apparatus by which images can be thrown on a plate sensitive to light.

se rene, placid; calm; clear.

ag ri cul'tur al, pertaining to the cultivation of land.

Word Building

Consult the dictionary for pronunciation and definition:

implement	platinum	exigency	innuendo
predatory	pernicious	assertion	felicitate

LESSON 79
Words Used in Business

en cy clo pe′di a, a summary of the whole field of knowledge.

vir′u lent (vĭr′-), extremely poisonous or venomous; deadly.

trans′it, passage through or over; transition.

an′thra cite, a kind of hard coal.

ex treme′, utmost; excessive; immoderate.

dis crim′i nate, to distinguish; to favor unfairly as against others.

coke, soft coal freed of volatile matter by heating in ovens.

de fi′ant, expressing resistance.

trav′es ty, a grotesque imitation; burlesque.

morgue (môrg), a place where the unknown dead are exposed for identification.

e ma′ci ate (-shĭ āt), to reduce in flesh; to make lean.

ex as′per ate, to irritate; enrage.

tes′ti mo ni al, a certificate attesting to one's character.

min′i a ture (-tŭr), represented on a small scale; a small portrait.

em pow′er, to give power to.

treas′ur er, one who has the care of a treasury or funds.

vouch′er, anything that confirms the truth of something.

ba rom′e ter, instrument for measuring atmospheric pressure.

un doubt′ed ly, without doubt or question.

de co′rous, becoming; proper; fit.

scru′pu lous, conscientious; careful; precise.

pla′gi a rize, to use as one's own the ideas, words, etc., of another.

mid′dle man, a dealer between the producer and consumer.

mis for′tune, bad fortune; mishap.

in cog′ni to (-nĭ tō), unknown; under an assumed name.

deb′it, to charge with a debt; an entry on the left-hand side of an account.

ul ti ma′tum, a final proposition; the last proposal or demand.

for′ty, thirty-nine and one more.

stal′wart (stôl′-), strong; muscular; of a sturdy build.

hyp′no tize (hĭp′-), to cause one to fall into a kind of sleep or trance.

le′ni ent, merciful; not severe.

u ni ver′sal, embracing or including the whole; unlimited.

Consult the dictionary for pronunciation and definition:

league	corporal	waybill	initiative
censor	mediator	option	mechanician

LESSON 80 (Oral)

Words ending in *er, or; sive, tive; tion, sion*

See Lesson 35 for the suffixes *or* and *er* and Lesson 42 for *tion* and *sion*.

af firm'	af firm'er	af firm'a tive	af fir ma'tion
ag gress'	ag gres'sor	ag gres'sive	ag gres'sion
ap pre hend'	ap pre hend'er	ap pre hen'sive	ap pre hen'sion
con trib'ute	con trib'u tor	con trib'u tive	con tri bu'tion
co-op'er ate	co-op'er a tor	co-op'er a tive	co-op er a'tion
cor rect'	cor rec'tor	cor rec'tive	cor rec'tion
dec'o rate	dec'o ra tor	dec'o ra tive	dec o ra'tion
de lib'er ate	de lib'er a tor	de lib'er a tive	de lib er a'tion
de stroy'	de stroy'er	de struc'tive	de struc'tion
dis trib'ute	dis trib'u tor	dis trib'u tive	dis tri bu'tion
ed'u cate	ed'u ca tor	ed'u ca tive	ed u ca'tion
il lus'trate	il lus'tra tor	il lus'tra tive	il lus tra'tion
in struct'	in struc'tor	in struc'tive	in struc'tion
in trude'	in trud'er	in tru'sive	in tru'sion
in vig'or ate	in vig'or a tor	in vig'or a tive	in vig or a'tion
nar rate'	nar ra'tor	nar'ra tive	nar ra'tion
op press'	op pres'sor	op pres'sive	op pres'sion
pos sess'	pos ses'sor	pos ses'sive	pos ses'sion
pro tect'	pro tec'tor	pro tec'tive	pro tec'tion
re mu'ner ate	re mu'ner a tor	re mu'ner a tive	re mu ner a'tion
re store'	re stor'er	re stor'a tive	res to ra'tion
se lect'	se lec'tor	se lec'tive	se lec'tion
spec'u late	spec'u la tor	spec'u la tive	spec u la'tion
suc cess'	suc ces'sor	suc ces'sive	suc ces'sion

Ag gress', to begin a quarrel or controversy; *ap pre hend'*, to arrest, to grasp mentally; *con trib'ute*, to lend aid to a common purpose; *co op'er ate*, to act jointly with another or others; *de lib'er ate*, to reflect on, not hasty or sudden; *dis trib'ute*, to divide among several or many; *il lus'trate*, to make clear, to adorn with pictures; *in trude'*, to force one's self in without invitation or welcome; *in vig'o rate*, to give vigor or life and energy to; *nar rate'*, to tell, relate; *re mun'er ate*, to repay, to compensate; *spec'u late*, to make a ventursome investment with hope of gain, to theorize, to meditate.

LESSON 81

Real Estate and Insurance

ac′tu a ry, one who computes insurance risks and premiums.

ten′e ment, a house or apartment for renting.

lease (lēs), to let by contract; a contract for renting property.

quit′claim, to relinquish or give up all title or claim.

de ben′ture, a written acknowledgment of a debt.

in dem′ni fy, to make restitution for loss, damage, etc.

bun′ga low, a one-story house.

mort ga gor′ (-jôr′), the person who gives a mortgage.

ten′ant, one who holds real estate by any kind of right.

chat′tel, any property except real estate.

sal′vage, insured property saved from fire.

ten′an cy, the period of a tenant's possession.

e ject′ment, a legal action for the recovery of lands, etc.

mor tal′i ty, number or rate of deaths.

sur ren′der, to give up possession of.

pre′mi um, sum paid for insurance.

ap pur′te nance, that which belongs to something else.

ap prais′al, the act of valuing or putting a price upon.

in her′it ance, property handed down by ancestors or others.

an nu′i ty, a series of equal payments made annually.

ac crued′, accumulated, as interest, rent, etc.

in dem′ni ty, remuneration for loss or damage.

oc′cu pan cy, state of occupying.

grant′or (tŏr; tôr′), the one by whom a grant is made.

re′al ty, real estate; landed property in any form.

les see′, one to whom a lease is given.

for′fei ture, act of forfeiting; a penalty.

front′age, extent of front, as of land along a street.

ben e fi′ci a ry, (-fĭsh′à rĭ), one received a benefit or advantage.

prem′i ses, a building or piece of land.

les′sor (lĕs′ôr; lĕs ôr′), one who grants a lease.

ab stract′, a summary; an epitome.

Consult the dictionary for pronunciation and definition:

fraudulent	foreclosure	mortgagee	legacy
participating	endowment	fee simple	tontine

LESSON 82

Law

ab scond', to leave secretly to avoid debt or legal process.

de po'nent, one who testifies under oath, especially in writing.

as sump'sit, an action to recover damages for breach of contract.

cod'i cil, a supplement to a will.

an'no tat ed, explained by written comments or notes.

gar nish ee', to attach property by law to pay a debt.

dock'et, an official record of court proceedings.

ap pel'late, relating to a court of appeal.

li'en (lē'ĕn; lēn), a legal claim on property.

in den'ture, a mutual agreement in writing.

void'a ble, capable of being annulled.

chan'cer y, a court of equity.

heir (âr), one who inherits property.

al'ien ate (āl'yĕn āte), to estrange or turn away.

tes'ta ment, a written declaration of one's last will.

ref er en'dum, the referring of a legislative act to the people for approval or rejection.

ar raign', to summon into court to answer an indictment.

cov'e nant, an agreement between two or more parties.

ar'son, the crime of maliciously setting fire to property.

lit i ga'tion, a judicial contest.

ac com'plice, an associate in the commission of a crime.

hom'i cide, the killing of one human being by another.

cli'ent, one who consults or employs a lawyer.

af fi da'vit, a sworn statement in writing.

he red'i ta ry, pertaining to an inheritance.

fi'at, an authoritative decree or command.

hei'nous (hā'nŭs), extremely wicked.

li'bel, a published slander.

ac ces'so ry, one who assists in the commission of a crime.

in dict' (-dīt'), to charge with an offense.

slan'der, a false, malicious report; to defame.

ci ta'tion, a summons to appear in court; a reference to a decided case.

Consult the dictionary for pronunciation and definition:

complainant	capias	larceny	rejoinder
adjudicate	abettor	alimony	claimant

LESSON 83

Law

de mur'rer, a plea of insufficiency of the cause of action.

de fend'ant, a person who is sued in a court of law.

no'ta ry, an officer empowered to administer oaths, etc.

in val'id, without force; null.

tort, any wrong for which a civil action can be brought.

ju ris dic'tion, legal authority; extent of power.

ten'ure, the period during which anything is held.

tres'pass, to intrude; to injure or annoy another.

pros'e cu tor, a public prosecuting attorney.

war'rant, to guarantee the title, quality, etc.

sit'u ated, located.

stat'u to ry, relating to statute law.

dom'i cile (-sĭl), a permanent residence.

ju'ror (-rẽr), a member of a jury.

ex tra di'tion, the surrender of an alleged criminal by one state to another.

sub poe'na (sŭb pē'nȧ), a writ commanding court attendance; to summon.

in tes'tate, without having made a will; one who dies intestate.

ju di'ci a ry, pertaining to courts or judicial procedure.

pro'test, a formal declaration of the nonpayment of a note, etc.

pet'it (pĕt'ĭ), small; insignificant.

tes'ti mo ny, a statement by a witness under oath.

de mur', to raise objections; to take exceptions.

mis de mean'or (-ẽr), any crime less than a felony.

cor rob'o rate, to make certain; to confirm.

de fal ca'tion (-făl-; dĕf'ȧl-), embezzlement.

war'ran ty (wŏr'-), a legal guarantee by the seller.

ver'sus, against.

jeop'ard y (jĕp'-), danger; hazard.

pa rol', not under seal, as a contract.

ver ba'tim, word for word.

man da'mus, a writ issued to enforce the performance of a public duty.

in junc'tion, a court order requiring a party to do or forbear some act; admonition.

Consult the dictionary for pronunciation and definition:

venue	perjury	plaintiff	interpreter
felony	self-defense	replevin	respondent

LESSON 84

Law

du ress', restraint of personal action by force or fear.

in cen'di a ry, pertaining to the malicious burning of property.

em bez'zle, to make private use of funds belonging to another.

im pan'el, to enroll upon a list for jury duty.

de pose', to testify under oath.

doc u men'ta ry, supported by documents.

in crim'i nate, to involve in a crime.

ir rel'e vant, not bearing on the case; extraneous.

quash, to set aside, as an indictment; to suppress forcibly.

wai'ver, act of relinquishing a right or privilege.

sum'mon, to command to appear in court.

con trac'tu al, of the nature of a contract.

dep o si'tion, written testimony under oath.

de cree', a judicial decision or judgment.

code, any systematic body of laws.

non'suit, to dismiss a case for lack of sufficient evidence.

ease'ment, any right that one may have in the land of another.

ju ris pru'dence, the science of law; a system of laws.

en join', to prohibit or restrain by judicial order.

for'ger y (fōr'-; fŏr'-), act of counterfeiting.

def a ma'tion, slander; libel.

sum'mons, a notice or command to appear in court.

tes ta'tor, one who leaves a will at his death.

ex ec'u tor, one appointed by a testator to execute his will.

pro'bate, official legal proof, as of wills.

ap pel'lant, one who appeals to a higher court.

mal fea'sance (-fē'zăns), official misconduct.

leg a tee', one to whom a legacy is bequeathed.

brief, a concise statement of the points of a legal argument.

in'quest, an official inquiry into the cause of a sudden death.

co re spond'ent, a joint respondent.

merg'er, a legal combination of two or more interests.

Consult the dictionary for pronunciation and definition:

rebuttal	certiorari	dower	assignor
assignee	recognizance	escrow	estoppel

LESSON 85

Automobiles

vac'u um, a space from which the air has been removed.

in'di ca tor, that which points out, as the hand on a gauge.

jour'nal, a bearing in which a shaft turns.

cou pe' (kōō pā'), a closed automobile for two persons.

bush'ing, a metal lining for a journal box.

ratch'et, a small toothed wheel.

el lip'tic, having the form of an ellipse.

crank'shaft, a shaft driven by a crank.

ig ni'tion, the device for exploding the charge in a gas engine.

graph'ite (-īt), a kind of carbon used as a lubricant, etc.

tax'i cab, a motor car for hire.

up hol'ster ing, interior fittings, as hangings, linings, etc.

pneu mat'ic (nū-), a rubber tire inflated with air.

disc, a flat, circular plate.

brough'am (brōō'um), closed automobile for four or five persons.

mag ne'to, a dynamo that generates the current in a gas engine.

speed om'e ter, an instrument for indicating speed.

tour'ing car, an open car for five or more passengers.

cyl'in der, the piston chamber of an engine.

bat'ter ies, apparatus for generating electricity.

de na'tured, changed in nature or character.

lu'bri cant, oil, grease, etc.

en am'el, to coat with a glossy composition.

com pres'sor, that which serves to compress.

dis trib'u tor, a device for distributing the electric current.

aux il'ia ry (ôg zĭl'yá rĭ), that which helps; aiding.

car'bon ize, to coat with carbon.

spark plug, a device in a gas engine for igniting the charge.

ex haust' (ĕg zôst'), the outlets leading from the cylinders.

cush'ion, a soft pad or pillow.

brake, a device for retarding or stopping by friction.

va na'di um, a rare element used in making a type of strong steel.

Consult the dictionary for pronunciation and definition:

radiator	commutator	throttle	countershaft
manifold	transmission	malleable	differential

LESSON 86

Automobiles

a lu′mi num, a silver-white metal noted for its lightness.

vi′bra tor, a device that produces vibration.

gas′o line, a volatile liquid.

clutch, a coupling for connecting two working parts.

chas′sis (shă′sĕ), frame, wheels, etc., of an automobile.

pet′cock, a valve to let air or water out.

a cet′y lene, an illuminating gas derived from calcium carbide.

vul′can ize, to harden rubber by heating and hammering.

au to mat′ic, self-acting.

ax′le, the spindle on which a wheel turns.

gas′ket, a packing used to make a water-tight joint.

coun′ter sunk, sunk even with or below the surface.

con dens′er, a device for compressing air or gases.

punc′ture, to pierce; a small hole.

sus pen′sion, the act of hanging from a support.

chauf feur′ (shō fûr′), one who is employed to operate an automobile.

ac ces′so ries, something additional and subordinate.

ac cel′er a tor, a device for increasing speed.

run′a bout, a light automobile.

pis′ton, a working part moving back and forth in a cylinder.

ton neau′ (tŏ nō′), afterbody of an automobile.

se dan′, a closed automobile having two seats.

li mou sine′ (lē mōō zēn′), a large automobile with inclosed top.

forge (fōrj), to form from metal by heating and hammering.

re verse′, turn backward.

gauge (gāj), an instrument for measuring.

muf′fler, a device for deadening noise.

ga rage′ (gȧ räzh′), a place for housing automobiles.

tax im′e ter, an instrument used in cabs for indicating fare.

bab′bitt, soft antifriction metal.

cy clom′e ter, device for recording revolutions of a wheel.

cam, a device for receiving or imparting motion to some part of a machine.

Consult the dictionary for pronunciation and definition:

carburetor	generator	dimmer	horse power
cantilever	transformer	gearing	micrometer

LESSON 87

Electrical Terms

e lec tri′cian, one skilled in electrical science.

de mag′net ize, to deprive of magnetic properties.

ar′ma ture, the revolving part of a dynamo.

an nun′ci a tor (-shǐ-), an electrical signaling device.

tel′e gram, a telegraphic message.

al′ter nat ing, said of a current that reverses rapidly.

ohm (ōm), the unit for measuring electrical resistance.

con′duit (-dǐt), a tube for electric wires, etc.

arc, light caused by the breaking of a current.

rhe′o stat, an apparatus for regulating an electric current.

e lec tric′i ty, an invisible force producing light, heat, etc.

in′su la tor, that which acts as a nonconductor of electricity.

cell, a single element of a voltaic battery.

ther′mal, relating to heat.

po lar′i ty, quality of having opposite poles.

e lec trom′e ter, an instrument for measuring differences of electric potential.

dy′na mo, a machine for producing electric current.

switch′board, an apparatus for connecting circuits.

ki net′ic, pertaining to or imparting motion.

cir′cuit (-kǐt), complete path of an electrical current.

in can des′cent, white with heat.

e lec′trode, either pole of an electric battery, etc.

West′ing house (George), inventor of the air-brake.

am pere′ (-pâr′), the unit of electrical current.

he′lix, a wire coil for conducting a current.

mag′net, a body having the power to attract iron.

tung′sten, a rare mineral element used in electric lamps.

am per′age (-pâr′-), the current strength in amperes.

gal van′ic, relating to chemical or voltaic electricity.

fil′a ment, a fibre or thread.

kil′o watt, a unit for measuring the power of an electric current.

vol tam′e ter, an instrument for measuring the quantity of electricity by means of electrolysis.

Consult the dictionary for pronunciation and definition:

insulate	**induction**	**ion**	**Marconi**
dynamic	**nonconductor**	**Edison**	**telegraph**

LESSON 88
Radio and Aviation

ra'di o, a general name for wireless telegraphy.

de tec'tor, device for detecting the presence of electric waves.

am'pli fi er, a device for increasing volume.

au di bil'i ty, quality of being audible.

an ten'na, wires for receiving or transmitting electric waves.

am'me ter, an instrument for measuring the amperage of a current.

por'ce lain, a hard insulating substance.

in ter fer'ence, intermixing of electric waves.

fre'quen cy, number of waves a second.

mi'cro phone, an instrument for amplifying or transmitting sound.

sen'si tive, capable of readily detecting radio impulses.

trans mit'ter, an apparatus for sending messages.

stat'ic, electrical disturbance in the air.

ra'di o phone, a wireless telephone.

wire'less, without use of wires.

re pro duc'er, a device that reproduces sound.

a vi a'tion, art or science of flying.

a ë'ri al, wires in the air to receive or radiate energy.

a'vi a tor, the driver or pilot of an airplane.

al'ti tude, vertical elevation; height.

par'a chute, a device for making a descent from an airplane.

al tim'e ter (ăl-), an instrument for indicating altitude.

mon'o plane, an airplane with one pair of wings.

an ti air-craft, a defense against aircraft.

fu'se lage, the body or frame of an airplane.

hy'dro-air'plane, an airplane that can light and glide on water.

bar'o graph, an instrument for registering altitude.

dir'i gi ble (dĭr'-), a balloon that can be directed.

bi'plane, an airplane having two supporting planes.

a ër o nau'tics, science of aërial navigation.

air'plane, a machine for flying.

py'lon (pī'lŏn), a guide post or tower on an aviation field.

Consult the dictionary for pronunciation and definition:

rectifier	radiogram	hangar	aëronaut
voltage	selectivity	airdrome	inclinometer

LESSON 89

Hardware and Lumber

as bes'tos, a fibrous mineral unaffected by fire.

pum'ice, a hard, light, spongy lava or rock.

wring'er, a machine for pressing water out of clothes.

cast'er, a small wheel on which furniture is supported.

car'tridge, a shell containing a charge for a gun.

pop'lar, a common forest tree.

scythe (sīth), an implement for mowing grass, etc.

fau'cet, a fixture for drawing a liquid from a pipe or vessel.

ma hog'a ny, a fine, ornamental hard wood.

mi'ter box, an apparatus for guiding a saw in cutting angles.

cut'ler y, edged or cutting tools collectively.

bev'el, an instrument for drawing angles.

butt, a kind of hinge.

zinc, a bluish-white crystalline metal.

cy'press, a species of evergreen tree.

rab'bet, a groove cut in the edge of a board to receive another member.

scis'sors, an instrument with two blades for cutting.

chis'el, a cutting-tool with a beveled edge.

swiv'el, a part that turns on a pin or headed bolt.

gal'van ize, to coat iron with zinc by means of heat.

shel lac', a gum used in making varnishes.

chest'nut, a kind of tree.

hick'o ry, a common nut-bearing tree and its wood.

sol'der (sŏd'ẽr), a metallic alloy used to join metal surfaces.

pin'cers, an instrument for gripping things.

re frig'er ant, any substance used in reducing temperatures.

tam'a rack, any species of the larch tree.

cal'i pers, instrument for measuring diameters.

syc'a more, a forest tree.

i'sin glass (ī'zĭn-), thin sheets of mica.

bronze, an alloy of copper and tin.

ve neer', to overlay with a thin surface of more valuable material.

Consult the dictionary for pronunciation and definition:

shears	shovel	wrench	cedar
sickle	funnel	walnut	buckle

LESSON 90 (Oral)

Words Ending in *tive, sive; tion, sion; able, ible*

See Lessons 32 and 33 for the suffixes *able* and *ible* and Lesson 42 for *tion* and *sion*.

VERBS	ADJECTIVES	NOUNS	ADJECTIVES
al'ter	al'ter a tive	al ter a'tion	al'ter a ble
de rive'	de riv'a tive	der i va'tion	de riv'a ble
laud	laud'a to ry	lau da'tion	laud'a ble
in vent'	in ven'tive	in ven'tion	in vent'i ble
cor rupt'	cor rup'tive	cor rup'tion	cor rupt'i ble
dif fuse'	dif fu'sive	dif fu'sion	dif fus'i ble
im ag'ine	im ag'i na tive	im ag i na'tion	im ag'i na ble
con nect'	con nec'tive	con nec'tion	con nect'i ble
de scribe'	de scrip'tive	de scrip'tion	de scrib'a ble
ex press'	ex pres'sive	ex pres'sion	ex press'i ble
e rad'i cate	e rad'i ca tive	e rad i ca'tion	e rad'i ca ble
ex haust'	ex haus'tive	ex haus'tion	ex haust'i ble
im press'	im pres'sive	im pres'sion	im press'i ble
ven'er ate	ven'er a tive	ven er a'tion	ven'er a ble
il lude'	il lu'sive	il lu'sion	il lu'sion a ble
re cu'per ate	re cu'per a tive	re cu per a'tion	re cu'per a ble
sug gest'	sug ges'tive	sug ges'tion	sug gest'i ble
con struct'	con struc'tive	con struc'tion	con struct'i ble
ac cu'mu late	ac cu'mu la tive	ac cu mu la'tion	ac cu'mu la ble
trans fuse'	trans fu'sive	trans fu'sion	trans fu'si ble
in tro duce'	in tro duc'to ry	in tro duc'tion	in tro duc'i ble
ob ject'	ob jec'tive	ob jec'tion	ob jec'tion a ble
sup press'	sup pres'sive	sup pres'sion	sup press'i ble
vi tu'per ate	vi tu'per a tive	vi tu per a'tion	vi tu'per a ble
de press'	de pres'sive	de pres'sion	de press'i ble

Laud, to praise highly; *diffuse,* to spread abroad, to circulate; *describe,* to give the characteristics of; *eradicate,* to root out, to exterminate; *exhaust,* to use up completely, to wear out by exertion; *venerate,* to regard with the highest respect, to revere because of age or wisdom; *illude,* to play upon by artifice, to deceive; *recuperate,* to regain health and strength; *accumulate,* to collect or bring together, to amass; *transfuse,* to pour out or transfer, as a fluid; *suppress,* to overpower, to repress; *vituperate,* to blame or censure abusively; *depress,* to press down, to sadden.

LESSON 91

Groceries and Provisions

as par'a gus, a plant used as a food.

mus'tard, a powder made of ground mustard seed.

ba na'na (bȧ nä'nȧ; bȧ năn'ȧ), a tropical edible fruit.

rai'sin, the dried fruit of the raisin grape.

vin'e gar, an acid; sour liquid.

cay enne' (kā ĕn'; kī ĕn'), a kind of pepper.

a'pri cot (ā'-; ăp'-), a fruit intermediate in flavor between a peach and a plum.

cin'na mon, an aromatic bark much used as a spice.

al'mond (ä'mŭnd), a tree and its nut.

ru ta ba'ga, a kind of turnip.

can'ta loupe (-lo͞op; -lōp), a kind of muskmelon.

spa ghet'ti (-gĕt'-), a variety of macaroni made in small cords.

mo'cha (mō'kȧ), a superior variety of Arabian coffee.

spin'ach (-ăj), a garden potherb.

bis'cuit (-kĭt), a small cake of bread; a cracker.

mac a ro'ni (-nĭ), an edible Italian paste of flour made into slender tubes.

res'tau rant, a public eating place.

gel'a tine, a jelly made from animal tissues.

may on naise' (mā ŏ nāz'), dressing for sauce or salad.

pump'kin, a vegetable vine and its fruit.

cel'er y, a garden vegetable.

hom'i ny, hulled corn prepared for food.

co'coa (kō'kō), ground seeds of the cacao or the beverage prepared from them.

caf e te'ri a, a restaurant where patrons serve themselves.

rhu'barb, pieplant; a medicinal root.

sal e ra'tus, cooking soda.

ca fe' (kȧ fā'), a restaurant or coffee house.

va nil'la, a flavoring extract obtained from the vanilla bean.

mar'ma lade, a preserve made of the pulp of fruit.

salm'on (săm'ŭn), a sea fish.

let'tuce (-ĭs), a garden plant used as a salad.

sal'ad, a preparation of vegetables, usually uncooked, served with a dressing.

Consult the dictionary for pronunciation and definition:

sugar	onion	sandwich	vegetable
ginger	radish	vermicelli	cranberry

LESSON 92

Dry Goods and Clothing

li no'le um, a kind of waterproof floor cloth.

mer'cer ized, treated chemically so as to resemble silk.

chev'i ot (chĕv'ĭ ŭt), a twilled woolen fabric.

cal'i co, a figured cotton cloth.

mack'in tosh, a waterproof outer garment.

tex'tile (-tĭl), a woven fabric or material for weaving.

cor'du roy, a coarse corded cotton fabric.

zeph'yr (zĕf'ẽr), a fine soft yarn.

cash'mere, a fabric made of fine wool.

cra ven ette' (krā-), a waterproof cloth.

ve lours' (vẽ' lōōr'), a woven fabric having a pile, or raised surface, like that of velvet.

skein (skān), a quantity of yarn, thread, etc., coiled together.

serge, a twilled woolen fabric.

hand'ker chief (hăn'kẽr chĭf), a pocket cloth or kerchief.

ho'sier y, stockings in general.

che nille' (shē nēl'), a kind of tufted cord used for trimming, fringes, etc.

rem'nant, an unsold end of a piece of cloth.

cas'si mere, a thin woolen cloth for men's garments.

me ri'no (-rē'-), a fine fabric of wool and cotton.

taf'fe ta, a lustrous silk fabric.

per cale', a smooth-finished cotton fabric.

den'im, a coarse cotton cloth used for overalls, etc.

dim'i ty, a kind of light cotton fabric.

gauze (gôz), a very thin fabric.

pop'lin, a corded fabric of many kinds.

ging'ham (-ăm), a kind of cotton or linen cloth.

wor'sted (wōōs'ted), a long-staple, firmly-twisted woolen yarn, and the cloth made from it.

chal'lis (shăl'ĭ), a light-weight cotton or wool cloth.

flan'nel, a soft woolen fabric.

or'gan die, a kind of fine thin muslin used for dresses.

wool'en, a cloth made from wool.

cham'bray (shăm'brā), a gingham woven in plain colors with linen finish.

Consult the dictionary for pronunciation and definition:

linen	**shoddy**	**braid**	**cretonne**
cravat	**overalls**	**muslin**	**toweling**

LESSON 93
Medicine and Diseases

rheu′ma tism, a painful disease of the joints, muscles, etc.

cap′sule, a soluble container for nauseous medicine.

al′um, sulphate of potassium and aluminum.

pneu mo′ni a, acute inflammation of the lungs.

nar cot′ic, a drug for producing sleep.

al′co hol, an intoxicating liquid.

bron chi′tis (-kī′-), inflammation of the bronchial tubes.

car bol′ic, pertaining to an acid obtained from coal tar.

ap pen di ci′tis (-sī′-), inflammation of the vermiform appendix.

strych′nine (strĭk′nĭn), a poisonous vegetable alkaloid.

co′ca ine (-ĭn; -ēn), a crystalline alkaloid used as an anaesthetic.

asth′ma (ăz′mȧ), chronic difficulty of breathing.

diph the′ri a (dĭf-), an acute disease of the throat.

hem′or rhage, profuse bleeding.

pto′ma ine (tō′mȧ ĭn), a substance found in decayed matter, sometimes highly poisonous.

an aes thet′ic (-ĕs-), a drug for producing insensibility to pain.

di ag nose′, to ascertain, as a disease, by its symptoms.

clin′ic, medical instruction by treatment before a class.

neu ral′gi a, an acute inflammation of a nerve.

tu ber cu lo′sis, a constitutional disease; consumption.

sur′ger y, healing by manual operation.

dys pep′si a, deranged digestion.

hy′gi ene (hī′gĭ ēn; hī′jēn), the science of health.

se′rum, the watery residue of an animal fluid after coagulation.

qui′nine, a drug prepared from the bark of the cinchona tree.

mor′phine (-fĭn; -fēn), a narcotic derived from opium.

ty phoid′, a fever marked by intestinal catarrh and ulceration.

vac′ci nate, to inoculate with a vaccine.

poul′tice, a soft application for sores or inflamed parts.

lau′da num, tincture of opium.

bo′rax, a crystalline compound used as an antiseptic and as a flux.

di ag no′sis, the determination of a disease from its symptoms.

Consult the dictionary for pronunciation and definition:

camphor	**pleurisy**	**glycerin**	**antitoxin**
catarrh	**liniment**	**benzine**	**disinfectant**

LESSON 94

Foreign Words and Phrases

Caution: Words marked with an asterisk to be written as two words.

en route (än rōōt'), on the way.

pro te ge' (prŏ tā zhā'), one under the care of another.

e lite' (ā'lēt'), a choice or very select social group.

fac sim'i le (-lē), an exact copy or likeness.

de bris' (dā brē'), rubbish, as remains from a wreck, etc.

in re (in rē), in the matter of.

*__per cap'i ta,__ by heads; for each individual.

re gime' (rā zhēm'), mode or system of government, social or political.

de luxe' (-lüks'), made with unusual elegance or luxury.

*__per cent',__ by the hundred; the interest, commission, or allowance on a hundred.

*__si'ne di'e,__ without setting a day for reassembling.

re su me' (rā zü mā'), a summary; an abridgment.

*__vi'ce ver'sa,__ in reversed order.

pas se' (pä sā'), worn out; faded.

*__no'ta be'ne,__ note well.

en core' (än kŏr'; än kōr'), a call for a repetition of a part of a play, etc.

*__per an'num,__ by the year.

*__pri'ma fa'cie__ (fā shĭ ē), at first view, as *prima facie* evidence.

*__ex of fi'cio,__ by virtue of the office; officially.

*__per di'em,__ allowance of so much by the day.

et cet'er a, and others of the same kind; and so forth.

*__per se,__ by itself; intrinsically.

fi na'le (fē nä'lā), the concluding part.

*__ca've at emp'tor,__ let the buyer beware; sold without guarantee.

*__bo'na fi'de,__ in good faith; genuine.

*__pro ra'ta__ (prō rā'tȧ), in proportion; as, the expense was shared *pro rata*.

ex po se' (-zā'), an exposure of something discreditable.

al'i bi (ăl'ĭ bī), fact of having been elsewhere at a given time.

fete (fāt), a festival; to feast.

ap ro pos' (-pŏ'), suitable to.

a'li as (ā'-), an assumed name.

pos se' (pŏs'ē), a body of men called by the sheriff to help make an arrest.

Consult the dictionary for pronunciation and definition:

petite	**extempore**	**ad infinitum**	**habeas corpus**
modiste	**rendezvous**	**postmeridian**	**nom de plume**

LESSON 95

New Words from the Addenda to Webster's New International Dictionary

de cel′er ate, to retard; to decrease velocity.

com mu ni que′ (kŏ mü nē kā′), an official communication.

cab ri o let′ (kăb rĭ ŏ lā′), an automobile resembling a coupé.

geor gette′ (jôr jĕt′), a kind of thin, silk crêpe.

graph′al loy, a substance used in making bushings, etc.

char meuse (shár mûz′), a soft fabric with a satin-like surface.

ca mou flage′ (ká mōō fläzh′), to disguise.

Czech′o-Slo vak′ (chĕk′ŏ slŏ văk′), a native of Czecho-Slovakia.

mar qui sette (mär kĕ zĕt′), a lustrous cotton or silk fabric.

no vo ca′ine (nō vŏ kā′ĭn), a kind of local anaesthetic.

fla′vine (-vĭn; -vēn), a kind of antiseptic.

de code′, to translate a code message into ordinary language.

Bol′she vism (bŏl′shĕ vĭz′m), doctrine of the Bolsheviki.

so viet′ (sō vyĕt′), a council largely identified with the Bolshevik movement.

prof it eer′, one who makes an unreasonable profit.

au to mo′tive, pertaining to machines that are self-propelling.

car bu re′tion (-rĕsh′ŭn), the act or process of carbureting.

nich′rome (nĭk′rōm), an alloy of nickel and chromium.

ac i do′sis (ăs ĭ dō′sĭs), a condition of acidity.

ba′ke lite, a hard substance used for insulating purposes.

cin′e ma′ (sĭn′), a moving picture; photoplay.

du ra lu′min (dū rá lū′mĭn), an alloy of aluminum, copper, etc.

du ve tyn′ (dōō vĕ tēn), any of several soft textile fabrics.

ra′di o graph, a picture obtained by means of invisible rays.

Bol′she vist, an adherent of Bolshevism.

lan dau let′ (lăn dô lĕt′), a brougham with a collapsible back.

lou′ver (lōō′vēr), openings in the side of an automobile hood.

cal′o rie (kăl′ŏ rĭ), unit used in expressing the fuel or energy value of food.

Word Building

Form adjectives ending in *able* or *ible* from the following words:

accept	permit	admit	contest
digest	profit	credit	commend
dispense	regret	collect	convert

LESSON 96 (Oral)

a chieve'	a chiev'ing	a chieve'ment	a chiev'a ble
com mit'	com mit'tal	com mit'ting	com mit'ment
con'fi dent	con'fi dent ly	con fi den'tial	con fi den'tial ly
con form'	con form'i ty	con'for ma tion	con form'a ble
ag'i tate	ag'i ta tor	ag'i tat ing	ag i ta'tion
de vote'	dev o tee'	de vo'tion	de vo'tion al
di late'	di lat'ing	di la'tion	di lat'a ble
di rect'	di rec'tor	di rec'to rate	di rec'tion
dis bar'	dis bar'ring	dis barred'	dis bar'ment
em'pha sis	em'pha size	em phat'ic	em phat'i cal ly
com mend'	com mend'a to ry	com men da'tion	com mend'a ble
es'ti mate	es'ti ma tor	es'ti mat ing	es ti ma'tion
ex treme'	ex treme'ly	ex trem'i ty	ex trem'ist
i den'ti fy	i den'ti fy ing	i den'ti fied	i den ti fi ca'tion
in form'	in form'er	in form'a tive	in for ma'tion
log'ic	log'i cal	log'i cal ly	lo gi'cian
nu tri'tion	nu tri'tious	nu'tri tive	nu'tri ment
o blige'	ob'li gate	ob'li ga to ry	ob li ga'tion
op'er ate	op'er a tor	op'er a tive	op er a'tion
pro fess'	pro fes'sor	pro fes'sion	pro fes'sion al
com mute'	com mut'ing	com mu ta'tion	com mut'a ble
reg'u late	reg'u la tor	reg u la'tive	reg u la'tion
sta'ble	sta'bil ize	sta'bi liz er	sta bil'i ty
trans late'	trans la'tor	trans la'tion	trans lat'ing
u til'i ty	u til i ta'ri an	u'ti lize	u ti li za'tion

Commit, to give in charge or trust, to perpetrate; *confident,* full of trust or certainty, positive; *conform,* to bring into harmony with, to comply; *agitate,* to stir violently; to excite; *dilate,* to expand or distend; *disbar,* to deprive of the right to appear in court as an attorney, to shut out; *commend,* express a favorable opinion of; *nutrition,* the process by which food substances are utilized, nourishment; *oblige,* to compel by force, to put under obligation to do or forbear something; *profess,* to declare openly, as one's belief, action, etc.; *commute,* to reduce the severity of; to pay in gross, at a reduced rate, as railroad fare; *regulate,* to adjust or control by rule or law, to put in order; *stable,* firmly established, durable; *translate,* to render into another language; *utility,* quality or state of being useful; *extremist,* a supporter of extreme doctrines or practices; *logician,* one skilled in the science of correct reasoning.

LESSON 97

Principal Cities of the United States

Ak'ron, Ohio
Al a me'da, Calif.
Al too'na, Pa.
Ashe'ville, N. C.
Ash ta bu'la, Ohio
Aus'tin, Texas
Ba'ton Rouge, La.
   (băt'ŭn rōozh)
Ba yonne', N. J.
Beau'mont, Texas
Berke'ley, Calif.
Beth'le hem, Pa.
Bev'er ly, Mass.
Boi'se, Idaho
   (boi'ză)
Butte, Mont.
Cam'den, N. J.

Char'lotte, N. C.
Chat ta noo'ga, Tenn.
Chel'sea, Mass.
Chic'o pee, Mass.
Cin cin nat'i, Ohio
Cleve'land, Ohio
Co hoes', N. Y.
Coun'cil Bluffs, Iowa
De ca'tur, Ill.
Des Moines', Iowa
   (dĕ moin')
Du buque', Iowa
   (dŏŏ būk')
Elk'hart, Ind.
El mi'ra, N. Y.
El Pas'o, Texas
E lyr'i a, Ohio

Eau Claire', Wis.
   (ō clâr')
E'rie, Pa.
Fond du Lac', Wis.
   (fŏn dŏŏ lăk')
Fort Wayne, Ind.
Fres'no, Calif.
   (frĕz'nō)
Glouces'ter, Mass.
   (glŏs-)
Ha'gers town, Md.
Ham tramck', Mich.
   (-trăm'ĭk)
Ha'ver hill, Mass.
   (Hā'vĕr ĭl)
Ha'zle ton, Pa.
Ho'bo ken, N. J.
Hol'yoke, Mass.

LESSON 98

Jo'li et, Ill.
Jop'lin, Mo.
Kal a ma zoo', Mich.
Kear'ny, N. J.
   (kär'-)
Ke no'sha, Wis.
La Crosse', Wis.
La re'do, Texas
   (Lá rä'dō)
Leb'a non, Pa.
Los An'gel es, Calif.
Lou'is ville, Ky.
McKees'port, Pa.
Mal'den, Mass.
Mer'i den, Conn.
Me rid'i an, Miss.

Mi am'i, Fla.
Mil wau'kee, Wis.
Min ne ap'o lis, Minn.
Mo bile', Ala.
   (mŏ bēl')
Mo line', Ill.
   (mŏ lēn')
Mont clair', N. J.
Mun'cie, Ind.
Mus ke'gon, Mich.
Mus ko'gee, Okla.
Nash'u a, N. H.
New Brit'ain, Conn.
New'burgh, N. Y.
New Ro chelle', N. Y.
   (shĕl')

Ni ag'a ra Falls, N. Y.
Nor'folk, Va.
Nor'wich, Conn.
Og'den, Utah
O kla ho'ma City, Okla.
O le an', N. Y.
O'ma ha, Nebr.
Osh'kosh, Wis.
Os we'go, N. Y.
Ot tum'wa, Iowa
Pa du'cah, Ky.
Pas a de'na, Calif.
Pas sa'ic, N. J.
Pat'er son, N. J.
Paw tuck'et, R. I.

LESSON 99

Pen sa co'la, Fla.
Pe o'ri a, Ill.
Perth Am'boy, N. J.
Phil a del'phi a, Pa.
Phoe'nix, Ariz.
  (fē'nĭx)
Pitts'burgh, Pa.
Pough keep'sie, N. Y.
  (pō kĭp'sĭ)
Pueb'lo, Colo.
  (pwĕb'lō)
Ra'leigh, N. C.
  (Rô'lĭ)
Ro'a noke, Va.
Sac ra men'to, Calif.
San An to'ni o, Texas
San Di e'go, Calif.
  (-dē ā'gō)

San Fran cis'co, Calif.
San Jo se', Calif.
  (-hŏ sā')
Sa van'nah, Ga.
Sche nec'ta dy, N. Y.
  (skē nĕk'tă dĭ)
Se at'tle, Wash.
Se da'li a, Mo.
She boy'gan, Wis.
Shen an do'ah, Pa.
Sioux Cit'y, Iowa
  (sōō-)
Som'er ville, Mass.
Spo kane', Wash.
  (-kăn')
Steu'ben ville, Ohio
Syr'a cuse, N. Y.

Ta co'ma, Wash.
Ter're Haute, Ind.
  (-hōt)
Tuc son', Ariz.
  (tōō sŏn')
Tul'sa, Okla.
U'ti ca, N. Y.
Val le'jo, Calif.
  (vă lā'hō)
Wal'tham, Mass.
Wich'i ta, Kans.
Wilkes'-Bar re, Pa.
Win'ston-Sa'lem, N. C.
Woon sock'et, R. I.
Worces'ter, Mass.
  (wōōs'-)
Zanes'ville, Ohio

LESSON 100

Alabama	Ala.	Nevada	Nev.
Arizona	Ariz.	New Hampshire	N. H.
Arkansas	Ark.	New Jersey	N. J.
California	Calif.	New Mexico	N. Mex.
Colorado	Colo.	New York	N. Y.
Connecticut	Conn.	North Carolina	N. C.
Delaware	Del.	North Dakota	N. Dak.
District of Columbia	D. C.	Oklahoma	Okla.
Florida	Fla.	Oregon	Oreg.
Georgia	Ga.	Pennsylvania	Pa.
Illinois	Ill.	Philippine Islands	P. I.
Indiana	Ind.	Porto Rico	P. R.
Kansas	Kans.	Rhode Island	R. I.
Kentucky	Ky.	South Carolina	S. C.
Louisiana	La.	South Dakota	S. Dak.
Maine	Me.	Tennessee	Tenn.
Maryland	Md.	Texas	Tex.
Massachusetts	Mass.	Vermont	Vt.
Michigan	Mich.	Virginia	Va.
Minnesota	Minn.	Washington	Wash.
Mississippi	Miss.	West Virginia	W. Va.
Missouri	Mo.	Wisconsin	Wis.
Montana	Mont.	Wyoming	Wyo.
Nebraska	Nebr.		

Alaska, Idaho, Iowa, Ohio, and Utah should not be abbreviated.
It is generally better not to abbreviate Maine and Oregon.

Two Hundred Demons

LESSON 101

(Selected from Lessons 1 to 40)

develop	secretary	specimen	prejudice
magnificent	malicious	budget	parcel
accommodate	miracle	balance	together
occurrence	compel	census	detriment
pamphlet	reference	fiscal	coincide
schedule	significant	prestige	accrued
transmitter	technical	censure	assure
apparatus	concede	anticipate	impair
noticeable	expense	across	adequate
changing	lieu	possess	embarrass
maintenance	business	deficit	supplement
advisable	separate	supersede	ventilator
preparation	privilege	despair	verify

LESSON 102

(Selected from Lessons 41 to 60)

recommend	gilt	imminent	convertible
disappoint	site	credible	prevalence
compliment	canvas	apparent	extravagant
precedent	lose	fallacy	circumstantial
unforeseen	waive	optimist	post-mortem
clientele	counsel	delicate	beneficiary
incentive	allege	incessant	disturbance
transient	merit	supremacy	collectible
beneficial	later	advisory	disbursement
extricate	serial	disparity	monotonous
principal	elicit	intercept	interchangeable
eliminate	devise	concession	immaculate
stationery	assessor	antiseptic	acquisition

Two Hundred Demons—*Con.*

LESSON 103

(Selected from Lessons 61 to 80)

exonerate	intricate	acumen	forbearance
grateful	fascinate	rescind	disseminate
acquiesce	scintilla	calendar	misinterpret
primarily	resistance	gratis	collateral
existence	extension	nickel	indebtedness
annoyance	equitable	abeyance	discrepancy
sacrifice	equivalent	sponsor	accelerate
congestion	exorbitant	lenient	negligible
consensus	consignor	tension	requisition
session	dimension	fickle	commensurate
definitely	grievance	salable	consummate
imitation	legitimate	demurrage	dissension
intrinsic	bulletin	exhilarate	authoritative

LESSON 104

(General Review, Lessons 1 to 99)

agitate	amateur	accidentally	benefited
tentative	accede	ridiculous	article
mediocre	ascertain	encumbrance	verbatim
Paterson	procedure	predicament	codicil
vicinity	comparison	comparative	asbestos
leisure	imperative	fraudulent	velours
souvenir	Cincinnati	miscellaneous	subpoena
mercantile	occurred	occasionally	jeopardize
effective	vertical	Schenectady	challis
colossal	prominent	interference	acquitted
emanate	chattel	permissible	affidavit
nuisance	chassis	phenomenal	pneumatic
endeavor	auxiliary	indispensable	Des Moines

VOCABULARY

A

abandon, 31
abatable, 25
abate, 25
abatement, 25
abbreviation, 45
abettor, 82
abeyance, 71
abhorrence, 70
abnormal, 2
abolish, 31
abominable, 32
abomination, 32
aboveboard, 68
abridgment, 25
abrogate, 63
abrupt, 47
abscess, 73
abscond, 82
absence, 8
absolutely, 76
absolve, 7
absorb, 59
absorbent, 70
absorption, 69
abstain, 23
abstinence, 23
abstract, 81
absurd, 2
abundance, 20
abundant, 20
abundantly, 20
abusive, 70
abutment, 66
abyss, 72
academic, 22
academy, 22
accede, 19
accelerate, 72
accelerator, 86
accept, 52
acceptable, 32
acceptance, 62
acceptation, 32
access, 3
accessible, 32
accession, 42
accessories, 86
accessory, 82
accident, 20

accidental, 20
accidentally, 20
accommodate, 6
accompanied, 38
accompaniment, 38
accompany, 38
accompanying, 38
accomplice, 82
accomplish, 7
accordance, 59
account, 33
accountable, 33
accountancy, 66
accountant, 66
accredit, 9
accrual, 25
accrue, 2
accrued, 81
accruing, 25
accumulable, 90
accumulate, 3
accumulation, 90
accumulative, 90
accuracy, 61
accurate, 61
accuse, 8
accustomed, 11
acetylene, 86
ache, 18
achieve, 41
acidosis, 95
acknowledge, 2
acknowledgment, 25
acme, 2
acoustic, 76
acquaint, 36
acquaintance, 70
acqueduct, 70
acquiesce, 62
acquire, 59
acquisition, 46
acquit, 28
acquittal, 28
acquitted, 28
acquitting, 28
acreage, 46
across, 8
actual, 47
actuary, 81
actuate, 47
acumen, 70

acute, 46
adage, 13
adapt, 52
adaptable, 33
addicted, 71
addition, 52
adept, 52
adequacy, 47
adequate, 4
ad infinitum, 94
adhere, 70
adherence, 54
adherents, 54
adhesive, 47
adjacent, 2
adjourn, 2
adjudicate, 82
adjunct, 7
adjure, 13
adjust, 35
adjustable, 33
adjuster, 35
administer, 73
administrator, 74
admirable, 32
admiration, 32
admire, 24
admiring, 24
admissible, 32
admission, 42
admit, 28
admittance, 28
admitted, 28
admitting, 28
admonish, 2
admonition, 47
adolescent, 70
adopt, 52
adorable, 32
adoration, 32
adult, 75
adulterate, 42
adulteration, 42
advance, 25
advancement, 25
advancing, 25
adventure, 59
adversary, 46
adverse, 14
adversity, 44
advertise, 35

advertiser, 35
advice, 52
advisable, 24
advise, 52
advisedly, 70
advisement, 60
adviser, 60
advising, 24
advisory, 59
advocate, 2
aerial, 88
aeronaut, 88
aeronautics, 88
affable, 33
affect, 52
affidavit, 82
affiliate, 5
affirm, 80
affirmation, 80
affirmative, 80
affirmer, 80
afflict, 59
affluence, 7
affront, 3
agency, 77
aggravate, 1
aggregate, 2
aggress, 80
aggression, 80
aggressive, 80
aggressor, 80
aggrieved, 7
agile, 21
agility, 21
agitate, 1
agony, 59
agree, 33
agreeable, 33
agricultural, 78
airdrome, 88
airplane, 88
aisle, 16
alcohol, 93
alert, 2
alias, 94
alibi, 94
alien, 26
alienate, 82
alienist, 62
alignment, 2
alimony, 82

allege, 60
allegeable, 60
alleger, 60
allegiance, 76
alleviate, 2
alley, 39
alleys, 39
alliance, 37
allies, 39
allowance, 37
allowed, 54
alloy, 70
allude, 42
allure, 47
allusion, 42
ally, 1
almighty, 19
almond, 91
almost, 19
alms, 17
aloud, 54
alphabet, 26
already, 19
altar, 55
alter, 55
alterable, 90
alteration, 90
altercation, 65
alternate, 65
alternating, 87
alternative, 44
although, 19
altimeter, 88
altitude, 88
altogether, 19
alum, 93
aluminum, 86
amalgamate, 68
amateur, 15
ambassador, 70
ambiguity, 22
ambiguous, 22
ambition, 43
ambitious, 43
ambulance, 11
ameliorate, 26
amenable, 33
amends, 70
American, 46
amicable, 70
ammeter, 88
ammonia, 75
amperage, 87
ampere, 87
amplifier, 88
amplify, 46
amuse, 25
amusement, 25
amusing, 25
anaesthetic, 93

analogous, 64
analysis, 65
analyze, 34
ancient, 44
anecdote, 63
anguish, 27
animated, 3
animosity, 66
annals, 2
anneal, 59
annex, 74
annihilate, 63
anniversary, 63
annotated, 82
announce, 25
announcement, 25
announcing, 25
annoyance, 62
annual, 12
annuity, 81
annunciator, 87
annonymous, 65
antecedent, 50
antedate, 50
antemortem, 50
antenna, 88
anteroom, 50
anthracite, 79
antiair-craft, 88
anticipate, 8
anticlimax, 50
antidote, 50
antimeridian, 50
antipathy, 50
antiquated, 68
antique, 27
antiquity, 44
antiseptic, 50
antithesis, 50
antitoxin, 93
anxiety, 12
anxious, 59
apathy, 59
apiece, 8
apologize, 34
apology, 10
appall, 47
apparatus, 30
apparel, 36
apparent, 59
appeal, 70
appear, 29
appearance, 29
appeared, 29
appearing, 29
appease, 10
appellant, 84
appellate, 82
append, 47
appendicitis, 93

appetite, 7
applaud, 47
applause, 6
appliance, 15
applicable, 67
applicant, 70
apportion, 59
appraisal, 81
appraise, 34
appraiser, 65
appreciable, 32
appreciate, 12
appreciation, 32
apprehend, 80
apprehender, 80
apprehension, 80
apprehensive, 80
apprentice, 68
apprise, 34
approbation, 44
appropriate, 6
approval, 24
approve, 1
approving, 24
appurtenance, 81
apricot, 91
apropos, 94
aptitude, 46
aqueduct, 70
arabesque, 27
arbitrary, 44
arbitrate, 42
arbitration, 42
arc, 87
architect, 26
archives, 26
arduous, 15
argument, 25
armature, 87
aroma, 75
arraign, 82
arrears, 3
arrival, 24
arrive, 24
arriving, 24
arrogant, 67
artisan, 62
arson, 82
article, 31
artifice, 43
artificial, 43
asbestos, 89
ascend, 62
ascertain, 22
asparagus, 91
aspect, 65
aspiration, 22
aspire, 22
assailant, 36
assay, 70

assertion, 78
assess, 60
assessable, 60
assessment, 60
assessor, 60
assets, 72
assign, 47
assignee, 84
assignor, 84
assistance, 52
assistants, 52
associate, 1
association, 61
assuage, 70
assumpsit, 82
assurance, 24
assure, 1
assuring, 24
asthma, 93
astonish, 46
astound, 7
astute, 1
asylum, 64
athletics, 70
atmosphere, 26
atom, 61
atrocious, 43
atrocity, 43
attack, 14
attain, 9
attainable, 33
attendance, 52
attendants, 52
attention, 65
attest, 46
attitude, 9
attorney, 77
attorneys, 39
attract, 46
attribute, 4
auctioneer, 47
audacious, 43
audacity, 43
audibility, 88
audible, 33
auditor, 63
auditorium, 59
auger, 55
aught, 54
augment, 46
augur, 55
auspicious, 70
austere, 65
authentic, 9
author, 34
authoritative, 65
authorize, 34
automatic, 86
automotive, 95
autumn, 37

auxiliary, 85
avail, 33
available, 33
avalanche, 15
avarice, 43
avaricious, 43
avenue, 10
average, 6
averse, 42
aversion, 42
aviation, 88
aviator, 88
avocation, 54
avoid, 33
avoidable, 33
avoidance, 71
awful, 25
axiom, 3
axle, 86

B

babbitt, 86
baggage, 44
bail, 55
baize, 16
bakelite, 95
balance, 10
bale, 55
ballot, 15
balm, 17
banana, 91
baneful, 75
banish, 3
bankrupt, 1
bankruptcy, 72
banner, 11
banquet, 6
baptize, 34
bare, 55
bargain, 70
barnacle, 31
barograph, 88
barometer, 79
barricade, 59
barrier, 2
barring, 44
barter, 59
basic, 14
basin, 4
basis, 9
batiste, 76
batteries, 85
bear, 55
beauteous, 38
beauty, 38
beckon, 4
bedrock, 61
beg, 28

beggar, 28
begged, 28
begging, 28
behavior, 75
behoove, 15
belated, 36
belief, 41
beliefs, 39
believable, 33
believe, 41
benediction, 59
benefactor, 61
beneficial, 43
beneficiary, 81
beneficent, 21
benefit, 21
benefited, 45
benevolence, 59
benevolent, 59
benignant, 75
benzine, 93
bequeath, 75
berth, 55
beseech, 59
besiege, 41
bespeak, 31
bevel, 89
beware, 5
bias, 11
bicycle, 50
biennial, 50
bier, 17
bimonthly, 50
bindery, 46
biplane, 88
birth, 55
biscuit, 91
bituminous, 65
blame, 25
blameless, 25
blaming, 25
bloc, 17
blot, 28
blotted, 28
blotter, 28
blotting, 28
bogus, 30
Bolshevism, 95
Bolshevist, 95
bona fide, 94
bonanza, 14
bonus, 30
bookkeeper, 72
borax, 93
borough, 74
boulevard, 71
bounteous, 38
bountiful, 63
bounty, 38
bouquet, 3

boycott, 1
braid, 92
brake, 85
brand-new, 66
braze, 17
brevity, 15
bribery, 59
brief, 84
briefs, 39
brilliant, 26
brochure, 78
brogue, 27
broker, 72
brokerage, 59
bronchitis, 93
bronze, 89
brougham, 85
brusque, 27
brutal, 21
brutality, 21
buckle, 89
buckram, 59
budget, 10
buffet, 74
bulletin, 70
bulwark, 59
bungalow, 81
buoy, 17
buoyant, 8
burden, 59
bureau, 10
burglary, 64
burlap, 75
burlesque, 27
burnish, 59
bury, 1
bushing, 85
business, 15
business like, 59
busy, 14
butt, 89

C

cabriolet, 95
cafe, 91
cafeteria, 91
calamitous, 38
calamity, 38
calendar, 75
caliber, 7
calico, 92
calipers, 89
calorie, 95
calumny, 65
cam, 86
cambric, 70
camera, 78
camouflage, 95
campaign, 8

camphor, 93
campus, 30
Canadian, 46
cancel, 29
canceled, 29
canceler, 29
canceling, 29
candid, 13
candidacy, 74
candor, 58
canoeing, 24
cantaloupe, 91
cantilever, 86
canvas, 55
canvass, 55
canvasser, 35
capias, 82
capital, 55
capitalist, 47
capitalize, 34
capitol, 55
caprice, 43
capricious, 43
capsize, 34
capsule, 93
captain, 74
caption, 15
carat, 53
carbolic, 93
carbon, 71
carbonize, 85
carburetion, 95
carburetor, 86
career, 14
caret, 53
cargo, 39
cargoes, 39
carriage, 5
carrot, 53
cartage, 13
carton, 54
cartoon, 54
cartridge, 89
cashier, 47
cashmere, 92
cassimere, 92
caster, 89
casual, 20
casually, 20
casualty, 20
catalogue, 27
catarrh, 27
catastrophe, 26
cater, 1
caucus, 30
caustic, 64
cauterize, 68
caution, 43
cautious, 43
caveat emptor, 94

cayenne, 91
cease, 23
cedar, 89
cede, 19
ceiling, 41
celebrate, 3
celerity, 74
celery, 91
celestial, 65
cell, 87
cellar, 71
celluloid, 75
cemetery, 71
censor, 62
censure, 9
census, 30
cent, 55
centennial, 78
center, 58
centuries, 39
century, 39
cereal, 55
certain, 22
certificate, 78
certify, 6
certiorari, 84
cessation, 23
chagrin, 28
chagrined, 28
chagrining, 28
challenge, 2
challis, 92
chambray, 92
chamois, 78
champion, 4
chancery, 82
change, 25
changeable, 67
changeless, 25
changing, 25
chaos, 21
chaotic, 21
chaperon, 78
character, 14
charge, 24
chargeable, 24
charging, 24
charitable, 33
charity, 33
charlatan, 68
charmeuse, 95
chassis, 86
chastise, 34
chattel, 81
chauffeur, 86
Chautauqua, 75
chemical, 67
chenille, 92
chestnut, 89
cheviot, 92

chief, 41
chiffonier, 74
chimney, 39
chimneys, 39
chisel, 89
chloroform, 26
choir, 55
choose, 52
chord, 17
chores, 7
chorus, 65
chose, 52
christen, 26
chronic, 26
chronicle, 67
chute, 16
cinch, 16
cinema, 95
cinnamon, 91
cipher, 66
circuit, 87
circuitous, 62
circular, 8
circularize, 34
circulate, 51
circumference, 51
circumstance, 43
circumstances, 51
circumstantial, 43
citation, 82
cite, 55
citizen, 12
civil, 40
civilian, 72
civility, 40
civilize, 40
civilly, 40
claimant, 82
clamor, 78
clarify, 5
classic, 68
classical, 31
classification, 38
classified, 38
classify, 38
classifying, 38
clause, 8
cleanliness, 38
cleanly, 38
cleanse, 17
clearance, 37
clemency, 64
clerical, 31
clever, 12
client, 82
clientele, 47
climax, 3
clinic, 93
clique, 27
cloth, 54

clothe, 54
clutch, 86
coalition, 74
coarse, 55
cocaine, 93
cocoa, 91
code, 84
codicil, 82
coerce, 6
coercion, 65
cogent, 70
cognizance, 67
coincide, 2
coincidence, 37
coincident, 67
coke, 79
collaborator, 45
collapse, 12
collapsible, 32
collapsion, 32
collateral, 72
colleague, 2
collect, 60
collectible, 32
collection, 32
collector, 60
collegiate, 78
collide, 42
collision, 42
colonial, 74
colonize, 34
colony, 34
color, 58
colossal, 11
column, 21
columnar, 21
comatose, 68
combustible, 32
combustion, 32
comfort, 33
comfortable, 33
comforter, 35
commemorate, 63
commendable, 32
commendation, 32
commensurate, 69
commerce, 43
commercial, 43
commission, 45
committee, 61
commodious, 65
commodity, 63
communicate, 63
communique, 95
commutator, 85
commute, 13
companies, 39
company, 39
comparable, 33
comparative, 23

compare, 33
comparison, 23
compatible, 33
compel, 19
compendium, 68
compensate, 10
compete, 22
competent, 59
competitive, 65
competitor, 22
compilation, 22
compile, 22
complainant, 82
complexion, 65
complement, 52
complete, 22
compliance, 38
complicate, 11
complies, 38
compliment, 52
comply, 38
complying, 38
component, 71
composite, 71
comprehensible, 32
comprehension, 32
compress, 35
compressible, 32
compression, 42
compressor, 85
comprise, 34
compromise, 34
comptroller, 78
compulsion, 65
compulsory, 66
compunction, 46
computation, 42
compute, 42
comrade, 64
conceal, 5
concealed, 45
concede, 19
conceit, 41
conceivable, 32
conceive, 41
concentrate, 2
conception, 32
concern, 8
concert, 13
concession, 42
conciliate, 15
concise, 6
conclude, 42
conclusion, 42
conclusive, 69
concrete, 5
concur, 28
concurred, 28
concurrence, 28
concurring, 28

condemn, 76
condense, 19
condenser, 86
condolence, 70
condone, 4
conduce, 22
conducive, 22
conduct, 35
conductor, 35
conduit, 87
confectioner, 22
confectionery, 22
confer, 28
conference, 28
conferred, 28
conferring, 28
confess, 35
confessor, 35
confidence, 20
confident, 20
confidential, 43
confidently, 20
confirm, 60
confirmable, 60
confirmation, 60
confirmer, 60
confiscate, 4
confuse, 42
confusion, 42
congenial, 70
congest, 9
congestion, 65
congratulate, 69
congregation, 69
congress, 75
conjecture, 11
connect, 90
connectible, 90
connection, 90
connective, 90
connivance, 7
connoisseur, 71
conquer, 9
copartner, 47
copartnership, 72
conscience, 66
conscientious, 65
conscious, 65
consecrate, 13
consecutive, 70
consensus, 65
consequence, 7
conservation, 22
conservative, 22
conserve, 11
considerable, 67
consideration, 67
consign, 13
consignee, 72
consignor, 72

consistency, 37
consolable, 32
consolation, 32
consolidate, 5
conspicuous, 65
conspiracy, 61
constituent, 36
construct, 90
constructible, 90
construction, 90
constructive, 90
construe, 11
consume, 35
consumer, 35
consummate, 70
contagion, 43
contagious, 43
contain, 35
container, 35
contaminate, 31
contemplate, 78
contemptible, 33
contend, 73
contention, 67
contiguous, 64
contingency, 37
contingent, 36
continual, 20
continually, 20
continuance, 22
continuation, 22
continue, 20
continuity, 69
contour, 70
contraband, 51
contract, 35
contractor, 35
contractual, 84
contradict, 2
contradictory, 70
contribute, 80
contribution, 80
contributive, 80
contributor, 80
control, 28
controllable, 33
controlled, 28
controller, 28
controlling, 28
controversy, 51
convalescent, 74
convene, 8
convenience, 26
conventional, 74
conversant, 22
conversation, 22
conversion, 60
convert, 60
converter, 60
convertible, 60

convey, 35
conveyance, 71
conveyor, 35
co-operate, 80
co-operation, 52
co-operative, 80
co-operator, 80
co-ordinate, 61
cope, 6
copied, 38
copious, 68
copy, 38
copying, 38
copyist, 38
copyright, 1
cordial, 15
corduroy, 92
core, 52
corporal, 79
corporation, 52
corps, 52
corpse, 52
corpulent, 75
correct, 80
correction, 80
corrective, 80
corrector, 80
correlate, 1
correspond, 70
correspondence, 52
correspondent, 84
correspondents, 52
corroborate, 83
corrode, 42
corrosion, 42
corrugated, 70
corrupt, 90
corruptible, 90
corruption, 90
corruptive, 90
costume, 64
cotton, 4
council, 55
counsel, 55
counseled, 29
counseling, 29
counselor, 29
counteract, 51
counterbalance, 51
counterclaim, 69
counterfeit, 41
countermand, 51
countershaft, 85
countersunk, 86
coupe, 85
coupon, 11
course, 55
courteous, 30
courtesy, 70
covenant, 82

covet, 4
cowardice, 78
cranberry, 91
crankshaft, 85
cravat, 92
cravenette, 92
create, 35
creative, 70
creator, 35
creature, 12
credence, 43
credentials, 43
credible, 33
creditable, 52
credulous, 64
cretonne, 92
crevice, 70
crisis, 36
critical, 40
critically, 40
criticism, 40
criticize, 58
crucial, 66
crucible, 33
crude, 16
cruelty, 63
cruise, 17
crux, 16
crypt, 17
crystal, 28
crystallize, 28
culinary, 70
culminate, 30
cultivate, 35
cultivator, 35
cumbersome, 63
cumulative, 71
curiosity, 31
curious, 70
currant, 55
currency, 11
current, 55
curriculum, 71
cursory, 37
curt, 18
curtail, 29
curtailed, 29
curtailer, 29
curtailing, 29
curtain, 3
cushion, 85
custodian, 21
custody, 21
custom, 5
customary, 61
customer, 59
cuticle, 45
cutlery, 89
cyclometer, 86
cyclone, 46

cylinder, 85
cymbal, 55
cynic, 14
cynical, 63
cypress, 89
Czecho-Slovak, 95

D

daintiness, 38
dainty, 38
dairy, 54
data, 2
dearth, 17
debase, 25
debasement, 25
debasing, 25
debatable, 33
debate, 33
debenture, 81
debit, 79
debris, 94
debtor, 77
debut, 77
decade, 7
decalogue, 27
deceit, 41
deceive, 41
decent, 54
deception, 68
decide, 42
decipher, 26
decision, 42
decisive, 15
declaim, 23
declamation, 23
declaration, 22
declare, 22
decode, 95
decorate, 80
decoration, 80
decorative, 80
decorator, 80
decorous, 79
decorum, 63
decree, 84
decrepit, 31
dedicate, 9
deface, 36
defalcation, 83
defalcator, 72
defamation, 84
default, 46
defective, 15
defendant, 83
defense, 58
defensive, 21
defer, 28
deference, 28

deferred, 28
deferring, 28
defiance, 38
defiant, 79
deficient, 44
deficit, 5
defies, 38
defile, 36
definite, 22
definitely, 66
defraud, 62
defunct, 3
defy, 38
defying, 38
degenerate, 71
degradation, 22
degrade, 22
delegate, 7
deliberate, 80
deliberately, 68
deliberation, 80
deliberative, 80
deliberator, 80
delicacy, 47
delicate, 68
delicious, 73
delineate, 72
delinquent, 61
delude, 42
deluge, 11
delusion, 42
deluxe, 94
demagnetize, 87
demagogue, 27
demeanor, 68
demise, 34
demolish, 3
demonstrable, 60
demonstrate, 60
demonstration, 60
demonstrator, 60
demoralize, 45
demount, 33
demountable, 33
demur, 83
demurrage, 72
demurrer, 83
denatured, 85
denim, 92
denomination, 74
departure, 47
depend, 33
dependable, 33
dependence, 37
dependent, 36
deplete, 7
deplorable, 63
deponent, 82
depose, 84
deposit, 4

deposition, 84
depositor, 77
depository, 59
depot, 10
deprecate, 74
depreciate, 4
depress, 90
depressible, 90
depression, 90
depressive, 90
deputy, 9
derelict, 66
deride, 42
derision, 42
derivable, 90
derivation, 90
derivative, 90
derive, 90
derogatory, 69
derrick, 73
descendant, 76
descent, 54
describable, 90
describe, 90
description, 90
descriptive, 90
desert, 55
design, 35
designate, 76
designer, 35
desire, 24
desiring, 24
desirous, 24
despair, 5
desperate, 77
despise, 63
despondency, 37
despondent, 70
dessert, 55
destination, 64
destitute, 46
destroy, 80
destroyer, 80
destructible, 32
destruction, 32
destructive, 80
detachable, 45
detect, 7
detector, 88
detention, 76
deteriorate, 64
detour, 73
detriment, 3
devastate, 64
develop, 1
deviate, 6
device 52
devise, 52
dexterity, 68
dexterous, 71

diagnose, 93
diagnosis, 93
diagonal, 74
dialogue, 27
diamond, 5
diary, 54
dictionary, 72
die, 24
differ, 29
differed, 29
difference, 29
different, 43
differential, 85
differing, 29
difficult, 37
diffuse, 90
diffusible, 90
diffusion, 90
diffusive, 90
digestible, 32
digestion, 32
dignify, 31
dignity, 4
digress, 12
digression, 42
dilapidated, 62
dilatory, 15
dilemma, 15
diligence, 37
diligent, 36
dilute, 9
dimension, 73
diminish, 21
diminution, 21
dimity, 92
dimmer, 86
dine, 29
dined, 29
diner, 29
dining, 29
diphtheria, 93
diploma, 11
diplomacy, 22
diplomat, 22
director, 75
directory, 46
dirge, 16
dirigible, 88
disagree, 48
disappear, 48
disappoint, 48
disaster, 23
disastrous, 23
disbursable, 60
disburse, 60
disbursement, 60
disburser, 60
disc, 85
discern, 5
discernible, 33

discipline, 9
discommode, 74
discordant, 72
discountenance, 65
discourteous, 62
discrepancy, 72
discretion, 23
discretionary, 71
discriminate, 79
discuss, 42
discussion, 42
disfranchise, 72
disguise, 34
disinfectant, 93
disinherit, 48
disintegrate, 64
disparage, 66
disparity, 59
dispatch, 58
dispel, 19
dispensation, 32
dispense, 19
disperse, 3
disseminate, 63
dissension, 67
dissent, 54
dissolution, 72
dissolve, 6
distill, 58
distinct, 2
distinguish, 27
distribute, 80
distribution, 80
distributive, 80
distributor, 58
disturb, 5
disturbance, 59
ditto, 3
diverge, 15
divers, 54
diverse, 54
diversion, 45
diversity, 30
divert, 3
divertible, 45
divest, 14
dividends, 72
divine, 24
divinely, 24
divinity, 24
divisible, 32
division, 32
divorce, 8
divulge, 14
docile, 11
doctrine, 4
document, 9
documentary, 84
domestic, 36
domicile, 83

dominant, 73
donate, 10
donor, 75
dormant, 73
dormitory, 59
dower, 84
draftsman, 58
drama, 40
dramatic, 40
dramatically, 40
dramatize, 40
drastic, 11
drawee, 47
drayage, 5
dream, 29
dreamed, 29
dreamer, 29
dreaming, 29
drudgery, 11
dual, 55
dubious, 12
duct, 18
ductile, 46
duebill, 72
duel, 55
duly, 25
dummy, 37
duplicate, 3
duplicator, 74
duplicity, 74
durable, 32
duralumin, 95
duration, 32
duress, 84
duteous, 38
duty, 38
duvetyn, 95
dyeing, 24
dying, 24
dynamic, 87
dynamite, 61
dynamo, 87
dynamos, 39
dyspepsia, 93

E

earnest, 1
easement, 84
eccentric, 68
echo, 26
eclipse, 76
economical, 40
economically, 40
economize, 40
economy, 40
ecstasy, 37
edible, 33
edict, 15
edifice, 15

Edison, 87
edition, 52
editor, 67
educate, 80
education, 80
educative, 80
educator, 75
efface, 4
effect, 52
effective, 10
efficacy, 76
efficient, 44
egotistic, 62
egotistical, 44
either, 41
eject, 2
ejectment, 81
elaborate, 3
elapse, 54
elastic, 13
elated, 1
electric, 20
electrical, 20
electrician, 87
electricity, 87
electrode, 87
electrometer, 87
elegance, 37
elegant, 36
elementary, 46
elevate, 35
elevator, 35
elicit, 52
eligible, 52
eliminate, 52
eliminator, 35
elite, 94
elliptic, 85
elucidate, 69
elude, 42
elusion, 42
emaciate, 79
emanate, 12
embargo, 72
embarrass, 4
embezzle, 84
embodiment, 12
emboss, 61
embroidery, 46
emerge, 51
emergency, 4
emigrate, 51
eminent, 52
emphasis, 26
emporium, 15
empower, 79
emulable, 60
emulate, 42
emulation, 42
emulative, 60

enact, 9
enamel, 85
encircle, 64
encompass, 78
encore, 94
encounter, 36
encourage, 3
encumber, 23
encumbrance, 25
encyclopedia, 79
endeavor, 15
endow, 6
endowment, 81
endurable, 60
endurance, 60
endure, 60
endurer, 60
enfranchise, 34
engrave, 12
engross, 3
enhance, 7
enjoin, 84
enjoy, 60
enjoyable, 60
enjoyer, 60
enjoyment, 60
enlarge, 25
enlargement, 25
enlarging, 25
enmity, 8
enormous, 30
enroll, 58
enroute, 94
ensemble, 77
ensuing, 5
entail, 75
enter, 23
enterprise, 34
enthusiasm, 10
enthusiastic, 63
entice, 78
entirety, 20
entitle, 3
entrance, 23
entwine, 58
envelope, 58
environment, 5
epidemic, 31
episode, 2
epitome, 78
epoch, 26
equal, 29
equaled, 29
equality, 29
equalize, 40
equally, 40
equilibrium, 66
equitable, 78
equity, 78
equivalent, 77

eradicable, 90
eradicate, 90
eradication, 90
eradicative, 90
erratic, 10
erroneous, 22
error, 22
escape, 25
escapement, 25
escaping, 25
escrow, 84
especial, 37
espouse, 14
essence, 43
essential, 43
estimable, 32
estimation, 32
estoppel, 84
et cetera, 94
ethical, 31
ethics, 13
etiquette, 74
eulogize, 44
eulogy, 37
evade, 42
evaluate, 73
evaporate, 35
evaporator, 35
evasion, 42
event, 20
eventual, 20
eventually, 20
evidence, 20
evident, 20
evidently, 20
evolve, 71
exaggerate, 10
exalt, 37
examine, 35
examiner, 35
exasperate, 79
excavate, 4
exceed, 19
excel, 19
excellence, 28
excellency, 28
excellent, 28
except, 52
exception, 33
exceptionable, 53
exceptional, 53
exceptionally, 20
excerpt, 8
excessive, 3
excise, 59
excitable, 24
excite, 24
exciting, 24
exclaim, 23
exclamation, 23

exclude, 42
exclusion, 42
exclusive, 73
excusable, 24
excuse, 24
excusing, 24
execute, 62
executive, 72
executor, 84
exemplary, 66
exemplify, 64
exempt, 3
exercise, 34
exhaust, 85
exhaustible, 90
exhaustion, 90
exhaustive, 90
exhibit, 6
exhilarate, 64
exhort, 12
exigency, 78
existence, 62
exit, 1
ex officio, 94
exonerate, 61
exorbitant, 72
expand, 60
expander, 60
expansible, 60
expansion, 60
expect, 53
expedient, 73
expedite, 9
expel, 19
expenditure, 73
expense, 19
expensive, 21
experience, 62
expiration, 22
expire, 22
explain, 23
explanation, 23
explanatory, 22
explicit, 1
exploit, 76
exponent, 36
expose, 94
ex-president, 51
express, 90
expressible, 90
expression, 90
expressive, 90
expulsion, 6
expunge, 66
exquisite, 14
extant, 8
extempore, 94
extension, 77
extenuating, 64
exterior, 61

exterminate, 44
extinct, 12
extinguish, 27
extinguisher, 45
extol, 75
extort, 66
extortion, 76
extract, 35
extractor, 35
extradition, 83
extraordinary, 51
extravagance, 77
extravagant, 45
extreme, 79
extricate, 51

F

fabric, 9
fabulous, 68
facile, 22
facility, 22
facsimile, 94
factor, 59
factories, 39
factory, 39
faculties, 39
faculty, 39
fair, 55
fallacious, 43
fallacy, 43
false, 17
falter, 12
familiar, 26
familiarity, 40
familiarize, 40
familiarly, 40
fanatic, 10
fare, 55
farther, 53
fascinate, 68
fashion, 3
fastidious, 73
fatal, 21
fatality, 21
fate, 55
fatigue, 27
faucet, 89
favorite, 7
favoritism, 47
faze, 18
feasible, 33
feat, 55
feature, 3
February, 61
fee simple, 81
feet, 55
felicitate, 78
felicity, 69
felony, 83

ferocious, 43
ferocity, 43
fertile, 21
fertility, 21
fete, 55
feud, 16
fiat, 82
fiber, 58
fickle, 71
fiction, 43
fictitious, 43
fidelity, 65
field, 41
fiend, 41
fierce, 41
fiery, 23
figuratively, 64
filament, 87
filch, 17
finale, 94
finance, 43
financial, 43
financier, 47
finite, 22
fire, 23
fiscal, 10
fixture, 4
flagrant, 30
flannel, 92
flavine, 95
flexible, 33
flourish, 11
fluctuate, 37
flux, 17
focus, 65
folio, 39
folios, 39
font, 17
forbear, 49
forbearance, 62
force, 25
forceful, 25
forcible, 33
forcing, 25
forebode, 49
forecast, 49
foreclose, 49
foreclosure, 81
forego, 49
foregoing, 61
foreign, 41
foresee, 49
foresight, 49
foretaste, 49
foretell, 49
forethought, 49
forfeit, 41
forfeiture, 81
forge, 86
forgery, 84

forlorn, 71
formal, 21
formality, 21
formally, 53
former, 1
formerly, 53
formidable, 33
formula, 7
forsake, 49
forth, 56
fortieth, 13
fortitude, 31
fortnight, 6
fortunate, 15
forty, 79
forum, 77
fountain, 6
fourth, 56
fragile, 73
fragrance, 37
fragrant, 37
franc, 17
franchise, 73
frantic, 1
fraternal, 75
fraudulent, 81
freight, 41
frequency, 88
friction, 44
friend, 41
frivolity, 21
frivolous, 21
frolic, 23
frolicking, 23
frontage, 81
frontier, 41
frugal, 21
frugality, 21
frustrate, 9
fugitive, 15
fulfill, 58
fullness, 58
fumigate, 42
fumigation, 42
function, 63
fundamental, 15
funeral, 5
funnel, 89
furious, 67
furniture, 14
further, 53
fuselage, 88
futile, 21
futility, 21

G

gaberdine, 74
galvanic, 87
galvanize, 89

garage, 86
garnishee, 82
gasket, 86
gasoline, 86
gaudy, 9
gauge, 86
gaunt, 18
gauze, 92
gazetteer, 69
gearing, 86
gelatine, 91
general, 34
generality, 40
generalize, 34
generally, 40
generator, 86
generous, 73
genial, 36
genius, 30
genuine, 65
geographic, 20
geographical, 20
georgette, 95
gesture, 36
gibe, 16
gigantic, 63
gilt, 56
ginger, 91
gingham, 92
gist, 16
glamour, 13
glisten, 5
glycerin, 93
gnash, 16
gorgeous, 74
governor, 65
gradually, 61
grammar, 21
grammatical, 21
granary, 62
grandeur, 11
granite, 7
grantor, 81
graphalloy, 95
graphic, 77
graphite, 85
grate, 56
grateful, 61
gratification, 38
gratifies, 38
gratify, 38
gratifying, 38
gratis, 73
gratitude, 73
gratuitous, 64
gratuity, 64
great, 56
grief, 41
grievance, 73
grotesque, 27

grudge, 18
guarantee, 73
guardian, 46
guest, 18
guilt, 56
guise, 45
gullible, 33
gymnasium, 71

H

habeas corpus, 94
haberdasher, 76
habit, 20
habitual, 20
habitually, 20
half-tone, 74
handicap, 28
handicapped, 28
handicapping, 28
handkerchief, 92
handsome, 6
hangar, 88
haphazard, 6
happily, 38
happy, 38
harass, 12
harmonious, 30
harmonize, 34
harmony, 34
hasten, 3
hastily, 38
hasty, 38
haughtily, 38
haughty, 38
havoc, 5
hazard, 2
healthful, 54
healthy, 54
heartily, 38
hearty, 38
height, 4
heinous, 82
heir, 82
helix, 87
helm, 18
hemorrhage, 93
hence, 16
herald, 13
hereditary, 82
heritage, 13
hermetically, 72
hero, 39
heroes, 39
heroism, 47
hesitancy, 22
hesitate, 22
hickory, 89
hideous, 46
hinder, 23

hindrance, 23
historical, 77
histories, 39
history, 39
hoard, 56
hoax, 17
hoeing, 24
holiday, 39
holidays, 39
homage, 10
homicide, 82
hominy, 91
honor, 58
honorary, 63
hope, 25
hopeful, 25
hopeless, 25
horde, 56
horizon, 5
horrible, 33
horror, 9
horse power, 86
hosiery, 92
hospitable, 33
hospital, 21
hospitality, 21
hostile, 21
hostility, 21
humbug, 28
humbugged, 28
humbugging, 28
humidity, 78
humiliate, 61
humility, 9
humor, 10
humorous, 30
hurricane, 36
hurriedly, 31
hydrant, 13
hydraulic, 75
hydro-airplane, 88
hygiene, 93
hyphen, 26
hypnotize, 79
hypothesis, 62

I

identical, 31
identify, 73
ignite, 60
igniter, 60
ignitible, 60
ignition, 85
ignoble, 48
ignoramus, 30
ignorance, 37
ignorant, 36
illegible, 52
illiberal, 48

invade, 42
invalid, 83
invalidate, 47
invasion, 42
inveigle, 41
invent, 90
inventible, 90
invention, 90
inventive, 90
inventory, 72
inversion, 32
invertible, 32
investigable, 60
investigate, 60
investigation, 60
investigator, 60
inveterate, 68
invigorate, 80
invigoration, 80
invigorative, 80
invigorator, 80
invincible, 33
invoice, 13
invoke, 4
involve, 9
iodine, 75
ion, 87
iota, 36
irksome, 71
irreconcilable, 32
irrefutable, 48
irrelevant, 84
irreparable, 48
irreproachable, 48
irresistible, 33
irrevocable, 67
irrigate, 10
irritable, 32
irritate, 10
irritation, 32
isinglass, 89
isolate, 5
issuance, 77
issue, 12
italic, 34
italicize, 34
item, 34
itemize, 34
itinerant, 36
itself, 6

J

janitor, 67
jealous, 64
jeopardize, 34
jeopardy, 83
jersey, 46
jewel, 29

jeweled, 29
jeweler, 29
jeweling, 29
journal, 85
journalize, 34
journey, 39
journeys, 39
jovial, 76
jubilant, 31
judgement, 25
judgment, 25
judicial, 43
judiciary, 83
judicious, 76
junction, 68
juncture, 75
junior, 65
jurisdiction, 83
jurisprudence, 84
juror, 83
justice, 43
justifiable, 67
justification, 38
justified, 38
justify, 38
justifying, 38
jute, 18
juvenile, 9

K

kerosene, 78
kidnap, 29
kidnaped, 29
kidnaper, 29
kidnaping, 29
kiln, 17
kiln-dry, 75
kilowatt, 87
kinetic, 87
kitchenette, 76
knack, 18
knife, 39
knives, 39
knotty, 6
knowledge, 2
kodak, 12

L

label, 29
labeled, 29
labeler, 29
labeling, 29
laboratory, 76
laborious, 45
lacerate, 74
lacquer, 76
ladies, 39
lading, 10

lady, 39
lamentable, 45
lamentation, 45
landaulet, 95
language, 27
languid, 27
languish, 27
lapse, 54
larceny, 82
last, 54
later, 53
latest, 54
lathe, 75
latitude, 4
latter, 53
laud, 90
laudable, 90
laudanum, 93
laudation, 90
laudatory, 46
launder, 12
laundry, 12
laurels, 14
lavatory, 71
lavish, 11
lax, 18
laxity, 46
leaf, 39
league, 79
lease, 81
leash, 18
leaves, 39
ledge, 18
leech, 18
legacy, 81
legal, 40
legality, 40
legalize, 40
legally, 40
legatee, 84
legible, 33
legion, 12
legislate, 35
legislator, 35
legitimate, 69
leisure, 7
leniency, 37
lenient, 79
lessee, 81
lessen, 56
lesson, 56
lessor, 81
lettuce, 91
level, 29
leveled, 29
leveler, 29
leveling, 29
libel, 82
liberal, 40
liberality, 40

liberalize, 40
liberally, 40
librarian, 46
license, 19
lie, 24
lien, 82
lieu, 16
life, 39
lightening, 54
lightning, 54
likelihood, 68
lilies, 39
lily, 39
limelight, 1
limit, 29
limitation, 29
limited, 29
limiting, 29
limousine, 86
lineal, 75
linen, 92
linguist, 27
liniment, 93
linoleum, 92
linotype, 75
liquefy, 23
liquid, 23
liquidate, 5
literal, 14
literary, 74
literature, 61
lithe, 18
litigation, 82
livelihood, 71
lives, 39
Lloyd's, 75
load, 29
loaded, 29
loader, 29
loading, 29
loaf, 39
loath, 54
loathe, 54
loaves, 39
local, 40
locality, 40
localize, 40
locally, 40
lodgement, 25
lodgment, 25
loiter, 4
loose, 53
lose, 53
louver, 95
loyal, 20
loyally, 20
loyalty, 20
lubricant, 85
lubricate, 35
lubricator, 35

lucid, 8
lucrative, 30
ludicrous, 66
luminous, 62
luncheon, 36
lurch, 16
luscious, 67
luster, 58
lustrous, 23
luxuriance, 37
luxuriant, 36
luxurious, 61
luxury, 10
lyceum, 46
lying, 24

M

macadamize, 75
machinist, 47
mackintosh, 92
magic, 20
magnet, 87
magnetic, 22
magnetism, 22
magnetize, 34
magneto, 85
magnificence, 37
magnificent, 36
magnify, 21
magnifying, 46
magnitude, 76
mahogany, 89
maintain, 23
maintenance, 23
majestic, 5
majority, 77
malfeasance, 84
malice, 21
malicious, 21
malignant, 76
malleable, 85
mammoth, 7
manage, 24
manageable, 24
managing, 24
mandamus, 83
maneuver, 75
manifest, 1
manifold, 85
manila, 58
manipulate, 35
manipulator, 35
manslaughter, 77
mantel, 56
mantle, 56
manual, 3
manufacture, 69
manuscript, 12
Marconi, 87

margin, 8
marmalade, 91
marquisette, 95
ma shal, 56
martial, 56
martyr, 14
marvel, 29
marveled, 29
marveling, 29
marvelous, 29
match, 39
matches, 39
material, 40
materiality, 40
materialize, 40
materially, 40
mathematical, 66
matriculate, 71
maturity, 69
maxim, 7
maximum, 14
mayonnaise, 91
mayor, 71
meager, 58
mean, 56
meat, 56
mechanic, 20
mechanical, 31
mechanically, 20
mechanician, 79
medal, 56
meddle, 56
mediator, 79
medical, 44
medicinal, 22
medicine, 22
mediocre, 5
medium, 11
meet, 56
megaphone, 76
melancholy, 26
memorandum, 15
memorize, 34
memory, 34
menace, 4
mental, 21
mentality, 21
menu, 8
mercantile, 8
mercenary, 64
mercerized, 92
merchandise, 34
merciful, 74
mere, 18
merge, 18
merger, 84
merino, 92
merit, 44
meritorious, 66
merrily, 38

merry, 38
metal, 56
metaphor, 74
mete, 56
meter, 58
method, 20
methodical, 20
methodically, 20
metropolis, 21
metropolitan, 21
mettle, 56
micrometer, 86
microphone, 88
microscope, 74
middleman, 79
mien, 56
mileage, 24
military, 21
militia, 21
millionaire, 61
mimic, 23
mimicked, 23
miner, 56
miniature, 79
minimize, 34
minimum, 5
minor, 56
minority, 22
minus, 30
miracle, 21
miraculous, 21
miscellaneous, 15
mischief, 41
mischievous, 30
misconstrue, 64
misdemeanor, 83
misfortune, 79
misinterpret, 64
misnomer, 61
misplace, 48
missent, 48
missile, 64
misspell, 48
misstate, 48
mistake, 33
mistaken, 48
miter, 58
miterbox, 89
mitigate, 15
mobile, 21
mobility, 21
mobilize, 75
mocha, 91
model, 29
modeled, 29
modeler, 29
modeling, 29
moderate, 35
moderator, 35
modernize, 44

modification, 38
modified, 38
modify, 38
modifying, 38
modiste, 94
mold, 58
momentary, 78
momentous, 19
momentum, 68
monetary, 22
money, 22
monkey, 39
monkeys, 39
monocle, 66
monologue, 27
monoplane, 88
monopolize, 34
monopoly, 34
monorail, 50
monotone, 50
monotonous, 50
moral, 40
morality, 40
moralize, 40
morally, 40
morgue, 79
morocco, 6
morphine, 93
mortal, 40
mortality, 81
mortalize, 40
mortally, 40
mortgagee, 81
mortgagor, 81
mortise, 58
mosque, 27
motto, 39
mottoes, 39
movable, 24
move, 24
moving, 24
mucilage, 64
muffler, 86
mulch, 16
multiplicity, 51
multiply, 51
multitude, 51
municipal, 21
municipality, 21
murmur, 1
muscular, 59
museum, 10
musical, 67
musician, 71
muslin, 92
mustard, 91
mutilate, 35
mutilator, 35
mutual, 40
mutuality, 40

mutualize, 40
mutually, 40
myrrh, 27
mysterious, 23
mystery, 7
mystify, 23
myth, 17

N

narcotic, 93
narrate, 80
narration, 80
narrative, 80
narrator, 80
national, 40
nationality, 40
nationalize, 40
nationally, 40
natural, 40
naturalization, 40
naturalize, 40
naturally, 40
naught, 54
nausea, 43
nauseous, 43
navigable, 60
navigate, 60
navigation, 60
navigator, 60
necessarily, 40
necessary, 40
necessitate, 40
necessity, 40
negative, 11
negligence, 37
negligent, 45
negligible, 33
negotiate, 72
neighbor, 41
neither, 41
nephew, 26
nervous, 30
neuralgia, 93
neutral, 40
neutrality, 40
neutralize, 40
neutrally, 40
nevertheless, 65
nicety, 20
niche, 16
nichrome, 95
nickel, 71
niece, 41
nineteenth, 13
ninetieth, 64
ninety, 44
ninth, 31
nom de plume, 94
nominal, 44

nominally, 62
nonarrival, 48
noncommittal, 48
nonconductor, 87
nonetity, 48
nonessential, 48
nonsense, 48
nonsuit, 84
normal, 1
nota bene, 94
notarial, 21
notary, 83
notice, 24
noticeable, 24
noticing, 24
notification, 38
notified, 38
notify, 38
notifying, 38
notoriety, 22
notorious, 22
nourish, 6
novelty, 3
novocaine, 95
nucleus, 30
nuisance, 14
null, 12
nullification, 38
nullified, 38
nullify, 38
nullifying, 38
numerate, 35
numerator, 35
numerical, 45
numerous, 76
nurture, 1

O

oar, 56
obdurate, 46
obedience, 37
obedient, 36
obey, 71
obituary, 68
object, 90
objection, 90
objectionable, 90
objective, 90
obligatory, 64
oblique, 27
obliterate, 69
obnoxious, 66
obscure, 24
obscuring, 24
obscurity, 24
observable, 60
observance, 76
observation, 22
observatory, 22

observe, 60
observer, 60
obsolete, 4
obstacle, 31
obstinate, 69
obviate, 9
obvious, 64
occasion, 20
occasional, 20
occasionally, 20
occupancy, 81
occupy, 10
occur, 28
occurred, 28
occurrence, 28
occurring, 28
oculist, 76
odious, 61
odor, 66
offense, 58
offensive, 21
office, 43
official, 43
officiate, 44
ohm, 87
omen, 23
ominous, 23
omission, 42
omit, 42
omnipotent, 62
omnipresent, 62
omniscient, 67
onerous, 64
oneself, 58
onion, 91
opaque, 27
opinion, 13
opponent, 36
opportune, 7
opportunity, 15
opposite, 3
oppress, 80
oppression, 80
oppressive, 80
oppressor, 80
optical, 67
optimism, 47
optimist, 47
option, 79
opulent, 75
orchestra, 26
ordeal, 7
ordinance, 54
ordnance, 54
ore, 56
organdie, 92
organize, 37
Orient, 12
origin, 21
original, 21

originate, 35
originator, 35
ornament, 1
orphan, 26
ostracize, 34
ought, 54
outcast, 49
outfit, 49
outgoing, 49
output, 49
outstanding, 49
outweigh, 49
ovation, 74
o'er, 56
overalls, 92
overbalance, 49
overcharge, 49
overdo, 49
overdraw, 49
overdue, 49
overhead, 49
overrate, 49
overseer, 49
overwhelm, 71

P

pacify, 30
pageant, 1
pair, 56
palace, 43
palate, 9
palatial, 43
pallid, 2
palpable, 33
pamphlet, 36
panacea, 30
panel, 14
panic, 23
panicky, 23
par, 8
parachute, 88
paradise, 34
paragraph, 26
parallel, 15
paralysis, 62
paralyze, 34
paramount, 9
parasite, 30
parcel, 4
pare, 56
parish, 14
parlor, 13
parochial, 26
parol, 83
parquet, 74
part, 43
partial, 43
participate, 61
participating, 81

particle, 31
particular, 31
partition, 53
pass, 33
passable, 33
passe, 94
passed, 56
past, 56
pasteurize, 68
pastor, 74
patent, 11
patentee, 47
pathetic, 7
patience, 76
patient, 44
patriot, 6
patrol, 9
patron, 34
patronage, 63
patronize, 34
pattern, 6
payee, 47
peace, 56
peak, 56
peal, 56
pear, 56
peculiar, 26
pecuniary, 61
pedagogue, 27
pedal, 56
peddle, 56
pedestal, 2
peek, 56
peel, 56
peer, 56
penalize, 62
pencil, 14
penetrable, 32
penetrate, 8
penetration, 32
penitent, 74
penitentiary, 59
pennant, 11
penniless, 30
penurious, 62
penury, 75
per annum, 94
percale, 92
per capita, 94
perceivable, 32
perceive, 50
per cent, 94
percentage, 76
perception, 32
perchance, 14
percolate, 50
percolator, 35
per diem, 94
peremptory, 73
perennial, 50

perfectible, 32
perfection, 32
perfidy, 4
perforate, 35
perforator, 35
perfunctory, 62
perilous, 30
period, 20
periodical, 20
periodically, 20
perish, 36
perjure, 77
perjury, 83
permanent, 73
permeate, 10
permissible, 32
permission, 42
permit, 42
pernicious, 78
perpetrate, 11
perpetual, 5
perplexity, 66
per se, 94
persecute, 54
perseverance, 73
persevere, 74
personal, 40
personality, 40
personalize, 40
personally, 40
personnel, 9
perspective, 11
perspiration, 22
perspire, 22
persuade, 42
persuasion, 42
pert, 18
pertain, 23
pertinent, 23
perusal, 63
peruse, 7
pervade, 50
pervert, 67
pessimism, 47
pessimistic, 44
pestilence, 74
petcock, 86
petit, 83
petite, 94
petition, 53
petroleum, 65
petty, 1
petulant, 36
phantom, 26
pharmacy, 26
phase, 26
phenomenal, 26
philosophy, 71
phonograph, 26
phosphate, 26

physical, 45
physician, 68
physique, 28
piano, 39
pianos, 39
picnic, 23
picnicker, 23
picturesque, 75
piece, 41
pier, 56
pierce, 41
pincers, 89
pinion, 26
pinnacle, 31
pioneer, 65
pique, 56
piston, 86
piteous, 38
pittance, 37
pity, 38
pivot, 4
placard, 46
plagiarize, 79
plague, 27
plaintiff, 83
plan, 28
planned, 28
planner, 28
planning, 28
plaque, 27
plastic, 37
plat, 14
platen, 13
platinum, 78
plausible, 73
pleasure, 47
pledge, 17
plenteous, 38
plenty, 38
pleurisy, 93
pliable, 67
plumb, 17
plunge, 18
plurality, 66
pneumatic, 85
pneumonia, 93
poignant, 69
poise, 10
polarity, 87
police, 11
policies, 39
policy, 39
polish, 12
polytechnic, 69
pomp, 30
pompous, 30
ponderous, 65
poplar, 89
poplin, 92
popular, 40

popularity, 40
popularize, 40
popularly, 40
porcelain, 88
porous, 30
portrait, 13
portray, 30
positive, 11
positively, 44
posse, 94
possess, 6
possession, 80
possessive, 80
possessor, 80
post date, 50
poster, 6
posterity, 62
postmeridian, 94
post-mortem, 50
postpone, 50
postscript, 50
posture, 46
potato, 39
potatoes, 39
potent, 43
potential, 43
poultice, 93
practicable, 53
practical, 31
praise, 18
precarious, 66
precede, 19
precedent, 53
precept, 6
precinct, 9
precious, 77
precipitate, 30
precise, 42
preclude, 73
precocious, 43
precocity, 43
predatory, 78
predecessor, 76
predicament, 8
predict, 9
predominate, 63
pre-eminent, 65
preface, 50
prefer, 33
preferable, 33
preference, 28
preferential, 43
preferred, 28
preferring, 28
prejudice, 4
prejudicial, 77
preliminary, 50
premature, 50
premier, 69
premises, 81

premium, 81
premonition, 69
prepaid, 50
preparation, 22
preparatory, 31
prepare, 22
preponderance, 62
preposterous, 67
prerogative, 69
presence, 54
presentable, 32
presentation, 32
presentiment, 50
presents, 54
preservation, 22
preservative, 22
preserve, 12
preside, 12
president, 53
presidential, 43
pressure, 5
prestige, 10
presumable, 32
presume, 32
presumption, 32
presumptuous, 19
pretense, 58 ·
pretension, 77
prevail, 23
prevalence, 45
prevalent, 23
prevaricate, 35
prevaricator, 35
previous, 30
prima facie, 94
primarily, 62
primary, 8
prime, 3
primitive, 31
principal, 53
principality, 20
principally, 20
principle, 53
prior, 21
priority, 21
privilege, 12
prize, 34
probate, 84
problem, 6
problematical, 69
procedure, 23
proceed, 19
process, 77
proclaim, 23
proclamation, 23
procrastinate, 68
prodigal, 15
prodigious, 76
prodigy, 11
produce, 60

producer, 60
producible, 60
production, 60
proffer, 1
professor, 67
proficient, 45
profile, 77
profit, 15
profiteer, 95
profuse, 42
profusion, 42
program, 64
progress, 77
prohibit, 14
project, 48
prolific, 68
prominence, 37
prominent, 74
promiscuous, 19
promissory, 69
promulgate, 72
prone, 16
pronoun, 48
proof, 39
proofs, 39
propel, 28
propelled, 28
propeller, 28
propelling, 28
propensity, 61
proper, 9
prophecy, 53
prophesy, 53
prophet, 26
propitious, 66
proportionate, 13
propose, 53
proprietor, 66
propriety, 61
pro rata, 94
prorate, 47
prosecute, 54
prosecutor, 83
prospective, 74
prospectus, 73
protect, 80
protection, 80
protective, 80
protector, 80
protege, 94
protest, 83
prove, 16
providence, 43
providential, 43
province, 43
provincial, 43
proviso, 39
provisos, 39
provocation, 77
provoke, 48

proximity, 64
proximo, 74
proxy, 72
prude, 16
prudence, 43
prudential, 43
psalm, 18
psychology, 65
ptomaine, 93
publicity, 63
pulley, 39
pulleys, 39
pulverize, 68
pumice, 89
pumpkin, 91
punctual, 20
punctuality, 20
punctually, 20
puncture, 86
purge, 16
purify, 31
purport, 2
purpose, 53
pursuance, 25
pursuant, 36
pursue, 25
pursuing, 25
pylon, 88

Q

quadruple, 71
qualification, 38
qualifies, 38
qualify, 38
qualifying, 38
quality, 11
qualm, 16
quantity, 37
quarrel, 29
quarreled, 29
quarreler, 29
quarreling, 29
quash, 84
quay, 17
query, 4
question, 33
questionable, 33
questionnaire, 78
quietus, 30
quinine, 93
quire, 55
quitclaim, 81
quiz, 16
quorum, 6
quota, 3
quotient, 44

R

rabbet, 89
radiant, 22
radiate, 22
radiator, 85
radio, 88
radiogram, 88
radiograph, 95
radiophone, 88
radish, 91
radius, 45
raiment, 8
rain, 57
raise, 57
raisin, 91
random, 9
ransom, 4
rap, 57
rapid, 21
rapidity, 21
rare, 25
rarely, 25
rarity, 25
ratchet, 85
ratification, 38
ratified, 38
ratify, 38
ratifying, 38
ratio, 37
rational, 63
ravage, 10
raze, 57
readjust, 49
real, 40
realization, 40
realize, 40
really, 40
realm, 16
realty, 81
ream, 18
rebate, 5
rebel, 64
rebuff, 4
rebuttal, 84
recall, 49
recapitulate, 49
recede, 19
receipt, 41
receivable, 33
receive, 41
receiver, 72
recent, 6
receptacle, 31
reception, 32
recipe, 1
recipient, 36
reciprocal, 31
reciprocate, 22
reciprocity, 22

reclaim, 23
reclamation, 23
recognition, 49
recognizance, 84
recognize, 77
recoil, 49
recollect, 49
recommend, 49
recompense, 49
reconcile, 49
reconciliation, 32
record, 15
recoup, 6
recourse, 11
recreation, 63
recruit, 77
rectifier, 88
rectify, 2
rectitude, 6
recuperable, 90
recuperate, 90
recuperation, 90
recuperative, 90
recur, 28
recurred, 28
recurrence, 28
recurring, 28
redeem, 32
redeemable, 32
redemption, 32
reduce, 73
reducible, 32
reduction, 32
re-enforce, 58
refer, 28
referee, 47
reference, 28
referendum, 82
referred, 28
referring, 28
refrigerant, 89
refrigerate, 35
refrigerator, 35
refusal, 9
refutation, 42
refute, 42
regenerate, 64
regime, 94
regiment, 3
register, 77
registrar, 46
regret, 33
regrettable, 33
rehabilitate, 77
rehearse, 12
reign, 57
reimburse, 49
rein, 57
reinstate, 63
reiterate, 61

rejoinder, 82
rejuvenate, 62
relapse, 54
relax, 8
release, 13
relevant, 61
reliance, 14
relic, 30
relies, 38
relief, 41
relieve, 41
religion, 43
religious, 43
relinquish, 30
relish, 9
reluctance, 37
reluctant, 36
rely, 38
relying, 38
remedy, 69
remember, 23
remembrance, 23
reminiscent, 75
remiss, 37
remission, 42
remit, 28
remittance, 28
remitted, 28
remitting, 28
remnant, 92
removal, 62
remunerate, 80
remuneration, 80
remunerative, 80
remunerator, 80
rendezvous, 94
renew, 10
renewal, 63
renounce, 12
renouncement, 45
renouncing, 45
renovate, 35
renovator, 35
repair, 23
reparation, 23
repeal, 4
repeat, 23
repeatedly, 14
repel, 19
repetition, 23
replenish, 5
replete, 2
replevin, 83
report, 35
reporter, 35
reprehensible, 32
reprehension, 32
representative, 63
repress, 42
repression, 42

reprieve, 41
reprimand, 31
reproducer, 88
repudiate, 42
repudiation, 42
repugnant, 76
reputable, 32
reputation, 32
require, 73
requisite, 66
requisition, 67
rescind, 69
rescue, 6
resent, 2
reservation, 62
reservoir, 14
residence, 43
residential, 43
residue, 10
resilient, 73
resistance, 77
resource, 1
respectfully, 53
respective, 14
respectively, 53
respite, 8
respondent, 83
response, 19
restaurant, 91
restoration, 80
restorative, 80
restore, 80
restorer, 80
restrain, 13
restrict, 13
résumé, 94
resurrection, 68
retain, 67
retaliate, 10
retention, 67
reticence, 37
reticent, 45
retire, 25
retirement, 25
retiring, 25
retort, 30
retrench, 47
retribution, 66
retrieve, 41
retroactive, 51
retrograde, 51
retrospectioɪ, 51
reveal, 7
revel, 29
reveled, 29
reveler, 29
reveling, 29
revenue, 10
reverse, 86
reversible, 32

reversing, 24
reversion, 32
revert, 67
review, 41
revise, 34
revival, 64
revoke, 5
rheostat, 87
rhetoric, 64
rheumatic, 27
rheumatism, 93
rhubarb, 91
rhythm, 27
riddance, 45
ridicule, 22
ridiculous, 22
right, 57
righteous, 61
rigorous, 67
rite, 57
rival, 12
rogue, 27
rôle, 57
roll, 57
rollic, 23
rollicking, 23
roster, 2
rostrum, 75
rotary, 72
rouge, 17
rout, 18
route, 18
routine, 77
royal, 20
royally, 20
royalty, 20
rudiment, 14
rue, 18
rummage, 8
rumor, 13
runabout, 86
ruse, 16
rusticate, 69
rutabaga, 91

S

sacrifice, 63
sacrilege, 67
sagacious, 45
salable, 75
salad, 91
salary, 13
saleratus, 91
salmon, 91
salutary, 44
salutation, 69
salute, 11
salvage, 81
salve, 18

Samaritan, 61
sanction, 62
sanctity, 68
sandwich, 91
sanguine, 27
sanitarium, 71
sanitary, 72
sarcastic, 68
satisfactorily, 38
satisfactory, 38
saturate, 12
scandal, 66
scarce, 20
scarcely, 20
scarcity, 20
scathing, 5
scene, 16
scenic, 9
scent, 55
schedule, 26
scheme, 26
schism, 18
science, 7
scientific, 63
scintilla, 69
scissors, 89
scoundrel, 8
scourge, 16
scrimp, 18
scrupulous, 79
scrutinize, 34
scrutiny, 34
scythe, 89
search, 18
secede, 19
seclude, 42
seclusion, 42
secondary, 46
secret, 22
secretarial, 62
secretary, 22
secular, 46
secure, 24
securing, 24
security, 24
sedan, 86
sedate, 7
sedentary, 65
sedition, 43
seditious, 43
seethe, 18
segment, 30
segregate, 2
seize, 41
select, 80
selection, 80
selective, 80
selectivity, 88
selector, 80
self-defense, 83

semblance, 14
semiannual, 50
semicircle, 50
seminary, 71
semiweekly, 50
senior, 65
sensitive, 88
sent, 55
sentinel, 14
separable, 60
separate, 15
separation, 60
separator, 60
sequel, 7
sequence, 8
serene, 78
serge, 92
sergeant, 65
serial, 55
series, 4
serious, 15
serum, 93
session, 66
severe, 20
severely, 20
severity, 20
sewer, 78
shale, 18
shape, 25
shapeless, 44
shapely, 25
shaping, 25
shear, 57
shears, 89
sheen, 18
sheer, 57
shelf, 39
shellac, 89
shelves, 39
sheriff, 69
shield, 41
ship, 28
shipped, 28
shipper, 28
shipping, 28
shirk, 17
shoddy, 92
shoeing, 24
shovel, 89
shrewd, 17
shriek, 41
sickle, 89
sight, 55
signal, 5
signature, 5
significance, 67
significant, 21
signify, 21
similar, 20
similarity, 20

similarly, 20
simplicity, 63
simplifying, 45
sincere, 20
sincerely, 20
sincerity, 20
sine die, 94
singeing, 24
singing, 24
singularly, 63
siphon, 26
sirup, 58
site, 55
situated, 83
size, 34
skein, 41
skeleton, 3
skeptical, 31
sketch, 16
slander, 82
sleigh, 41
sleight, 57
sleuth, 17
slight, 57
slogan, 59
slough, 16
sluice, 16
slur, 18
smuggle, 13
society, 61
sojourn, 6
solace, 13
solder, 89
sole, 57
solemn, 40
solemnity, 40
solemnize, 40
solemnly, 40
solicit, 14
solicitor, 76
solicitous, 63
solitary, 13
solo, 39
solos, 39
solution, 2
solvency, 37
solvent, 36
soul, 57
source, 16
souvenir, 8
sovereign, 41
Soviet, 95
space, 43
spacious, 43
spaghetti, 91
sparkplug, 85
sparse, 16
spasmodic, 61
special, 40
specialize, 40

specially, 40
specialty, 40
specie, 9
specific, 4
specification, 38
specified, 38
specify, 38
specifying, 38
specimen, 11
spectacle, 31
speculate, 80
speculation, 80
speculative, 80
speculator, 80
speedometer, 85
sphere, 26
sphinx, 18
spinach, 91
spindle, 31
splendor, 10
splurge, 16
sponge, 16
sponsor, 72
spontaneous, 44
spurious, 65
spurn, 17
squelch, 17
stable, 53
staid, 17
stake, 57
stalwart, 79
stamina, 5
stampede, 9
stanch, 18
standard, 34
standardize, 34
staple, 53
state, 25
statement, 25
static, 88
stating, 25
stationary, 53
stationer, 22
stationery, 22
statistician, 65
statue, 53
stature, 53
status, 30
statute, 53
statutory, 83
steak, 57
steal, 57
steel, 57
stencil, 59
stenographer, 61
sterilize, 74
sterling, 1
stigma, 3
stimulant, 22
stimulate, 22

stimulus, 30
stipulate, 42
stipulation, 42
storage, 74
straight, 57
strait, 57
strange, 25
strangely, 25
strangeness, 25
stratagem, 23
strategic, 23
strenuous, 64
strict, 22
strictly, 22
stringency, 37
stringent, 36
strychnine, 93
studio, 39
studios, 39
studious, 66
stupefy, 23
stupendous, 19
stupid, 21
stupidity, 21
sturdy, 15
suave, 17
subagent, 50
subdivision, 50
subdue, 62
subjugate, 50
submersible, 32
submersion, 32
submission, 42
submit, 42
submitting, 45
subordinate, 50
subpoena, 83
subside, 1
subsidiary, 72
subsidize, 34
subsidy, 34
substance, 43
substantial, 43
substantiate, 62
substitute, 2
suburban, 46
suburbs, 14
succeed, 19
success, 80
succession, 80
successive, 80
successor, 80
succinct, 68
succor, 8
succumb, 7
suede, 18
suffice, 4
sufficient, 44
suffrage, 12
sugar, 91

suggest, 90
suggestible, 90
suggestion, 90
suggestive, 90
suite, 57
summarize, 34
summary, 34
summon, 84
summons, 84
sumptuous, 19
sundries, 47
sundry, 47
superabundant, 51
superb, 12
superficial, 45
superfluous, 51
superintendent, 36
superior, 63
supersede, 19
superstition, 43
superstitious, 43
supervise, 34
supervisor, 77
supplement, 15
supplementary, 44
support, 35
supporter, 35
supposable, 32
suppose, 32
supposition, 32
suppress, 90
suppressible, 90
suppression, 90
suppressive, 90
supremacy, 47
supreme, 13
sure, 7
surety, 20
surfeit, 41
surgery, 93
surgical, 31
surmise, 34
surplus, 6
surprise, 34
surrender, 81
survey, 35
surveyor, 35
susceptible, 33
suspect, 53
suspend, 76
suspense, 19
suspension, 86
suspicion, 43
suspicious, 59
sustain, 23
sustenance, 23
swath, 17
sweet, 57
switchboard, 87
swivel, 89

sycamore, 89
symbol, 55
symmetrical, 69
symmetry, 21
sympathetic, 66
sympathize, 34
sympathy, 34
synagogue, 27
synonym, 22
synonymous, 22
syndicate, 37
system, 40
systematic, 40
systematically, 40
systematize, 40

T

tabernacle, 45
tacit, 12
tact, 16
tactics, 3
taffeta, 92
talent, 1
tamarack, 89
tangible, 33
tare, 57
tariff, 1
tarnish, 11
taunt, 17
taut, 17
taxicab, 85
taximeter, 86
tear, 57
technical, 31
technique, 27
tedious, 63
telegram, 87
telegraph, 87
temporary, 8
tenable, 33
tenacious, 43
tenacity, 43
tenancy, 81
tenant, 81
tendency, 9
tender, 8
tenement, 81
tenet, 13
tenor, 14
tension, 67
tentative, 5
tenure, 83
terminal, 47
terminate, 15
terminus, 30
terrible, 33
territory, 9
terse, 16

testament, 82
testator, 84
testimonial, 79
testimony, 83
textile, 92
texture, 5
theater, 58
their, 57
theoretical, 20
theoretically, 40
theories, 39
theorize, 40
theory, 20
there, 57
therefor, 52
therefore, 52
thermal, 87
thief, 39
thieves, 39
thorough, 7
threshold, 14
throe, 17
throttle, 85
thwart, 16
thyme, 17
tie, 24
tincture, 6
tinge, 2
tingeing, 24
tinging, 24
tithe, 16
title, 36
to, 57
toeing, 24
together, 2
toleration, 32
tomato, 39
tomatoes, 39
tongue, 27
tonnage, 72
tonneau, 86
tontine, 81
too, 57
topic, 46
toque, 27
tornado, 39
tornadoes, 39
tort, 83
total, 14
touring car, 85
tournament, 1
toweling, 92
trace, 24
traceable, 24
tracing, 24
tract, 4
tractor, 75
tragedies, 39
tragedy, 23
tragic, 23